THE INFALLIBLE FORTUNE TELLER

THE
INFALLIBLE
FORTUNE
TELLER

A romantic memoir

JOHN GOODALL AND
MAHIN RASHVAND

T

The manufacturer's authorised representative in the EU for product safety is Authorised Rep
Compliance Ltd, 71 Lower Baggot Street, Dublin D02 P593 Ireland
(www.arccompliance.com)

Troubador Publishing Ltd
Unit E2 Airfield Business Park,
Harrison Road, Market Harborough,
Leicestershire. LE16 7UL
Tel: 0116 2792299
Email: books@troubador.co.uk
Web: www.troubador.co.uk

ISBN 978 1836283 119

British Library Cataloguing in Publication Data.
A catalogue record for this book is available from the British Library.

Printed and bound in Great Britain by 4edge Limited
Typeset in 11pt Minion Pro by Troubador Publishing Ltd, Leicester, UK

This book is dedicated to the memory of two unknown souls who are believed to have met in northern Iran during the eleventh or twelfth century. A young woman of good birth by chance met and fell in love with a young man from a different culture. But because the young woman was destined for an arranged marriage, this love match was never to be fulfilled. Such was the strength of their affections that before parting they made a solemn vow to hold on to that love forever. Consequently, they went their separate ways, their love for one another frustrated until the day they died.

The book is offered in recognition of that solemn vow and presented as evidence that their love for one another has since been fulfilled as recounted in this book.

AUTHORS' FOREWORD

This memoir is presented as a work of creative non-fiction. The first duty of writers of memoirs to their readers is to convey the truth. Where this book is concerned, this point is of cardinal importance. For this reason, I have taken great care to ensure that this narrative correlates with the relevant events, most of which unfolded in 1969. That said, there is inevitably a large amount of detail that is impossible to accurately recall after such a lapse of time. In this regard I would stress the word 'creative'. To make the narrative more enjoyable for the reader, I have endeavoured to bring our story to life, presenting it more like a novel through recounting many of the events in the form of dialogue. My wife, Mahin, had no direct involvement in drafting this manuscript. Her dialogue was drafted by my ghost writer, Josephine Galvin.

Not all conversations will have occurred at the time and places suggested and, in some instances, they constitute a reconstruction of various themes my wife and I discussed in subsequent years. I also feel bound to explain that

Mahin's command of English all those years ago was not as impressive as the narrative may infer. Rather, her story has been reconstructed from her explanations.

My decision to publish this memoir has been taken with some reluctance. Romantic stories - even if based on truth - are usually published as fiction. Only in the most exceptional circumstances would anyone choose to publish the most intimate episodes of their private lives. Down the years, Mahin and I have recounted this story to numerous friends and acquaintances and seen it received with expressions of near disbelief followed by pleas for its publication. Finally, I feel obliged to relent and publish!

Since the Iranian revolution of 1979, very few people have dared visit Iran if only for political or security reasons. Yet contrary to common perception the Iranians have for centuries been well-known for their hospitality and tradition of welcoming strangers. I hope that this book will enable the reader to appreciate - if not completely understand - the often infuriating idiosyncrasies of the eclectic, conflictual, enigmatic, perplexing and frequently misunderstood nation that was - and hopefully still is - modern-day Iran.

In some instances, it has not been possible to accurately recall from memory the names of certain characters for which I apologise.

John Goodall
June 2025

PROLOGUE

Anyone who knows, and knows that he knows,
Makes the steed of intelligence leap over the vault of heaven.
Anyone who does not know, but knows that he does not know,
Can bring his lame little donkey to the destination nonetheless.
Anyone who does not know, and does not know that he does not know
Is stuck for ever in double ignorance.

Anonymous but attributed to Naser od-Din Tusi (1201–1274)

Tehran 1967
Mahin:

It was entirely Tahira's idea. Azar had agreed but with reticence, being somewhat nervous to learn her destiny, whereas I was more concerned as to how much money this supposed fortune teller was going to charge. But we were close friends and attended the same college. And, who knew, it could possibly be an entertaining way to spend the afternoon.

It was a particularly hot day, making the street even

more sultry than usual. I hadn't realised how far away it was – we had walked for almost an hour already, which was quite wearing in our high heels. Tahira had initially been very talkative, overexcited, as she enthused about the Assyrian woman we were about to meet. She had it on good authority that this woman was never wrong, and she recounted the details of an exciting fortune a friend of hers had received. The more she enthused, the more cynical I found myself becoming, until we settled into a silence to conserve our energy in the heat.

However, as we reached the steps of the rather nondescript house, I felt my heartbeat quicken, and I was glad I was holding hands with my friends.

I am not sure which of us rang the bell, but I don't think any of us took a breath as we waited for the door to open. I think I was shaking, which was unlike me.

Eventually we heard the lock being turned and found ourselves facing the woman that was reputed to be able to read our destinies. Of middle age, but looking older due to her gaunt frame, she had black, waist-length hair tied in plaits, a prominent nose and rather wizened skin. Her long green dress seemed almost a costume. She certainly looked the part.

'Appointment?' Her voice managed to be simultaneously both suspicious and indignant.

Both Azar and I looked at Tahira.

'Err … I'm afraid not. Should we have called first?' Tahira looked back at us.

'Sorry, I didn't know.'

'Clients should book first. I am here alone with my cat.

If I'm interrupted in the middle of a seance, everything is ruined.'

She looked furious, and I was sure she was going to turn us away. I was half relieved and half dreading the long walk back with our disappointed friend. Then she appeared to have a change of heart.

'Never mind, you're here now. You'll have to wait, though, as I am doing a reading.'

She indicated that we should follow her, and with a brief exchange of glances, we allowed ourselves to be shown to some chairs in the hallway, after which she disappeared down a dimly lit corridor and up the stairs at what must have been the back of her house.

We sat in silence, relieved to be cooling off within the thick walls. I looked around and noticed a large wooden crucifix hung on one of the walls, and below this the smoke of incense curled upwards towards the ceiling. Like most Assyrians in Iran, the members of this household were clearly affiliated to the Chaldean Catholic Church. There was little else to look at, and as the minutes passed, I found myself getting irritated again.

'This is a waste of time. I bet this is part of her plan – we are kept waiting for so long that we happily part with a significant sum of money when we are eventually seen. And it's all just a bundle of lies. I think we should leave.'

As if I had somehow willed it, there was the sound of feet on the stairs, and the man we assumed to be the first client appeared. He was muttering to himself, and as he reached us, he looked in our direction, yet he clearly was in some kind of trance.

'It's amazing, absolutely amazing …'

I felt myself swallow hard. The woman was back, and in silence she gestured us to follow her upstairs. Instinctively, we reached for each other's hands.

The room into which she led us was clearly kept intentionally dark. The windows were all covered; the small shafts of light that escaped through curtain gaps reassured us that it was still daylight outside this claustrophobic cell. The walls were lined with tapestries – each one depicting strange scenes of humans and beasts. The only furniture was a small table and the surrounding chairs, in which, she indicated, we should sit. She placed herself opposite us. In the centre of the table was a globe lamp, and from its open top a tiny column of smoke curled towards the ceiling. There was no going back now.

She looked at each one of us in turn, yet I felt she lingered longest on my face. I felt strangely nervous.

'Who sent you here?'

We looked at Tahira. Her reply was faltering.

'Er … just a college friend.'

The woman appeared to be waiting for a name, but Tahira continued, 'You told her a wonderful fortune. She has not stopped bragging about it. I… I mean we… hoped ours would be the same.'

'Fortunes are personal to you. I read what I see. I can't guarantee it will be wonderful.'

She asked us our names as she sprinkled some incense onto the lamp. It flickered, then brightened, sending a thicker column of smoke above our heads.

'My fee is 25 tomaans (about $3.50.)'

'Each?' I'd been expecting she would try something like this.

'Yes – each!'

'That's ridiculous. A rip-off!'

Tahira shifted uneasily in her chair whilst glaring at me. She clearly wanted to proceed.

'Mahin, you don't have to do it. You can just wait for us. You'll do it, won't you, Azar?'

Before Azar could answer, the fortune teller intervened.

'If all three of you accept, I'll accept a reduced payment of 20 tomaans each. I do have my reputation to consider.'

For the sake of my friends, I swallowed my inclination to get up and leave. All three of us handed over our notes.

The woman gathered the notes and disappeared behind a heavy curtain. We could hear the rattle of crockery before she emerged with three small cups of Turkish coffee, which she placed in front of each of us.

She then proceeded to rub an old oil lamp with an embroidered cloth before touching the wick with a lighted taper. Putting it back on the table, she opened the palms of her hands towards the ceiling, closed her eyes and uttered a supplication to a djinn. Finally, she clapped her hands forcefully and began to shuffle a pack of cards. Once these cards were thoroughly shuffled, she spat on the pack and dealt three cards to each of us.

'Pick up the top card and turn it over, face up on the table.'

We did as she commanded.

'Now drink the coffee in one gulp and immediately turn the empty cup upside down on its saucer.'

Looking at each of us in turn, she peered into the globe in the centre of the table and then dealt another single round of cards. 'Now turn the card I've just dealt face up and place it next to the first one.' She paused, then added, 'Now turn your coffee cups the right way up.'

The fortune teller leaned forward to examine the grounds in the bottom of each cup, and while doing this she picked up our remaining cards and turned them over.

Her expression changed almost immediately as she uttered a little shriek. She appeared horrified by something. I looked at my friends, and they both looked alarmed by this change in her composure.

'This is absolutely terrible! I can't possibly tell your fortunes – it's out of the question. I may be able to tell Mahin's but not Azar's or Tahira's. They're just too horrible!'

Tahira looked confused and upset. She found the confidence to protest.

'But I insist! And besides, we've paid you already.' I looked at Azar, who appeared frozen with shock.

'No problem, I will refund your money.'

Azar interjected, 'No! I want to know what you saw. I need to hear it.'

'There are some truths that you should never hear.' The fortune teller was gathering the cards away as if to bring the session to an end.

'Please!' cried Azar. 'If I leave here now without knowing what is to become of me, my life will be a misery. I'll be sick with worry.'

'Me too,' Tahira added, more quietly than her friend.

The fortune teller shrugged her bony shoulders.

'Take my advice; take your money back. I am not happy to disclose unhappy outcomes. I will tell Mahin's fortune only.'

'That's quite intolerable,' Tahira interjected. 'I insist! At least if I know, then I'll understand what to be concerned about rather than worrying about anything and everything.'

'Sometimes it is preferable to be ignorant.' She began getting their money from the pocket in her dress.

Tahira and Azar appeared crestfallen and, looking at one another, sought solace in their common predicament. Then Azar took the lead. 'Both Tahira and I agree, you must keep your word and tell our fortunes.'

There was a long pause as the fortune teller drew her breath.

'Very well then. If you insist, I'll tell you, but you must understand that it's against my better judgement, and I take no responsibility for the consequences.'

Addressing each of us in turn, she began.

'Azar, you're going to have a terrible accident, almost certainly a car accident. It won't be fatal, but it risks leaving you badly scarred for life.' She turned to Tahira.

'Tahira, you're going to lose someone very close to you, and it seems it may happen quite soon.' Ignoring the alarm on Tahira's face, she turned to look at me.

'Mahin, I'm quite convinced that you'll be very fortunate, and I can clearly foresee that three things will happen. Firstly, something will come into your name. Secondly, you'll meet a man with blond hair and blue eyes. And thirdly, you'll travel the world.'

We were all silent as we considered her words. I tried

to suppress my excitement at what I had just heard. It would surely have been in awful taste to look pleased after the terrible fortunes my friends had been given. We just looked at each other in amazement. The chime of the doorbell downstairs pierced our shock. We stood up to leave, and I politely thanked the fortune teller for her prediction for me. I walked behind my friends as they descended the stairs and waited for the woman to unbolt her door. Her waiting client stood aside as we stepped outside into the glaring light of the afternoon.

Standing in the street, I could see how despondent my companions looked. I felt compelled to play it down.

'Utter rubbish, what a load of stuff and nonsense! Didn't you see how she looked at the grounds in the bottom of my coffee cup and declared that she could see a man with blond hair and blue eyes in there? It's just not serious. For heaven's sake let's go home and forget all about it. If you two believe all or any of that nonsense, you'll both get utterly depressed.'

'It's all very well for you, Mahin, but what about us?' Tahira countered bitterly. 'I did tell you that she has a truly remarkable reputation – at the Royal Court even – for getting it right. After all you've heard and what's been said, it's no use trying to palm us off with denigrating remarks about stuff and nonsense in coffee grounds. Did you see her face? That was genuine anguish, not playacting. I think we just have to accept that everything we've heard will come true.'

'Well, in that case, maybe you shouldn't have brought us here in the first place,' I added unhelpfully. 'It was your idea, after all.'

'Shut up, both of you!' Azar exclaimed. 'Believe what you will, but I know what I'm going to do: until I have a serious accident, I shall drive my car no faster than 20 kilometres an hour.' She turned and walked off ahead of us. I realised she needed to be on her own.

I began to walk back slowly with Tahira. We were quiet as we left that fateful street: lost in our own thoughts and each dealing with our differing destinies. I played the fortune teller's prediction for me over and over in my mind. A man with blond hair and blue eyes…

'How could that ever be true in this city? There simply aren't any.'

Tahira looked at me, and I realised I had spoken aloud. She smiled for the first time since coming out of that strange house.

'Well, that's OK, even if you never actually meet him, at least you can lie in bed at night and – err… well – let's politely say, dream about him.'

'Now don't get personal!'

But Tahira was just too distracted to listen to any more of my thoughts, and I didn't wish her to think me insensitive. Placing my arm around her shoulder, I tried to offer some comfort:

'Just don't worry about it. Believe me, it's all nonsense. Come on, let's get a taxi home.'

1

MY FAMILY GARDEN OF PARADISE

Be happy for this moment. This moment is your life.

Omar Khayyam

Life in Ghazvin in the years following the Second World War
Mahin:

The city of Ghazvin is situated on the old Silk Road that runs westward from Tehran towards Tabriz and Turkey. Briefly the capital city of ancient Persia in the 16th century, it has seen the comings and goings of invading armies, while in medieval times its population, like that of so many Iranian cities, was decimated by the Mongols. It owes its existence to an important crossing of caravan trails, since it is from here that travellers heading west must choose between continuing on towards Tabriz and Turkey or turning right across the mighty Alburz mountains towards the Caspian Sea. Indeed, it is said that the name *Ghazvin* or *Qazvin* is a corruption of the word *Caspian,* while many *Ghazvinis* consider that the Caspian Sea takes its name from that of their ancient city.

Yet another road leads in a north-easterly direction, winding its way up into the High Alborz to the ancient mountain fortress of Alamut. It was here in the 11th century that my famous ancestor, Hasan-i-Sabah, established the headquarters of the *Ismailis*, known in the west as the *Assassins*, the world's first political terrorists. Centuries later, after passing through Ghazvin, Marco Polo returned to Europe with terrifying tales of political assassinations. In his book, titled *Travels*, published in the latter years of the 13th century, he wrote:

> *Hasan-i-Sabah, the founder of a deadly enigmatic Islamic sect that came to be known in Europe as the Assassins, had made in a valley between two mountains the biggest and most beautiful garden that was ever seen, planted with all the finest fruits in the world and containing the most splendid mansions and palaces that were ever seen, ornamented with gold and with likenesses of all that is beautiful on earth, and also four conduits, one flowing with wine, one with milk, one with honey and one with water. There were fair ladies there and damsels, the loveliest in the world...*

Whether or not that garden in fact existed has been disputed ever since, but there is little doubt that the story was widely believed in Europe at the time. This is borne out by the fact that the word *assassin* can be found in most European languages though, strange to say, not in Persian.

Together with my brothers and sisters, I spent many of my childhood years in such a walled garden at our home in Ghazvin. It embraced a rectangular plot of land measuring some 50x100 metres. The garden was configured in the traditional Zoroastrian way, being divided into four sections representing respectively earth, fire, water and air. These sections were divided by streams and pathways. According to the Koran, a garden of paradise is served by four fountains, one producing wine, another water, another milk and the last one honey. In our garden, in addition to a spring flowing from the next-door premises, we did indeed have a goat producing milk, grapes for wine and beehives producing honey, while in the centre of the garden was a swimming pool.

Our family house, located at one end of the garden, was laid out on just two floors. Our living accommodation was on one floor, under a flat roof, and beneath this there was a semi-basement for storage. The exterior walls were clad in stone, but from an architectural standpoint, the building was unremarkable. Within these walls, my mother had given birth to 12 children, including two sets of twins. Only three boys and four girls survived into adulthood. A large family requires a lot of space, and we certainly had it here. The house boasted several reception rooms and numerous bedrooms, and the basement was huge. At harvest time our basement was stacked high with all kinds of produce in preparation for winter: pistachios, almonds, olives and walnuts. All these treats were stored in large wooden barrels. Sacks of wheat harvested from the family estates were piled high on wooden platforms so that vermin could not reach them. Dried fruit such as raisins, sultanas, tomatoes and the like that had been drying on the flat roof in the summer were similarly conserved in large stoneware vats, their necks stuffed with muslin gauze and sealed with a layer of wax. Sharif Abad, a village close to Ghazvin, was famous for the cultivation of watermelons, and unsurprisingly one section of the basement was piled high with melons that would last until springtime. Shut away in a partitioned corner of the cellar, we stored wine made from grapes harvested from my mother's extensive vineyards.

In another corner was a bread oven. This was used just twice a year when a team of bakers would visit to bake bread. My mother, an only child, had inherited most of the local windmills around Ghazvin. The arrival of the bakers was preceded by the delivery of several sacks of wheat to one of these local mills for grinding into flour. The kind of bread they baked was called *lavache*. Being very thin, it could be kept dry for long periods and revived prior to eating by simply sprinkling it with a few drops of water. The bread once baked was stacked up in piles and wrapped in large linen sheets and stored on wooden shelves suspended from the ceiling. More vats still were filled each year with imported white cheese purchased in the bazaar. To make the cheese more palatable, it was first mixed with various herbs, each vat being labelled according to its contents, before also being sealed with wax.

It was a childhood pleasure to sneak into the basement unsupervised. Once there, I would uncover a labyrinth of stored delights and could feast on the nuts and dried fruits. Yet it was breathing in the mix of delicious aromas, in this sensory paradise, that most lingers in my memory.

With the arrival of electricity, it became possible to incubate large batches of fertilised chickens' eggs. Once old enough, the chicks were moved to a large coop in one of the corners of the garden, thus providing our family with an adequate supply of meat and eggs throughout the year.

In addition to cultivating a variety of vegetables, the garden boasted numerous fruit trees: apple, apricot, plum, almond and even pomegranate and pistachio. The stream – fed from a spring in a nearby property – entered the garden through a hole in the perimeter wall. From there, it ran through the middle of the garden, feeding irrigation channels as it progressed, and then entered the swimming pool at one end. From where it exited the pool, it continued around the garden before disappearing through a second small opening in the perimeter wall at the opposite end. In this manner the stream was used to irrigate the gardens of numerous properties in the neighbourhood. Near the pool stood two enormous trees, one a walnut tree that was estimated to produce as many as 30,000 nuts every year and the other a mulberry tree that yielded huge quantities of white mulberries. High up in one of those trees a suspended steel tank provided running water to the house. At the bottom of the garden was an annex that housed the servants' quarters.

In this part of Iran there are effectively just two seasons: summer and winter. As it is located some 1,800 meters above sea level, the summers are hot and dry, whilst the winters are bitterly cold and bring heavy falls of snow. Following each snowfall, flat roofs had to be cleared to reduce the extra weight as well as to ensure that no water seepage occurred during the thaw. Labourers would throw the snow in all directions, but the largest volume amassed on one side, which by winter's end could reach a height greater than the house itself. Our father would make use of this to bury and preserve wild fowl, whilst we children much preferred to enjoy it as a toboggan slope.

I recall many winters walking to school with the snow piled high on each side of the footpaths. There were no school meals in those days, so we were allowed a two-hour break to return home for lunch. Given that it was 40 minutes' walk each way, we spent three and a half hours a day walking to and from school! We barely had time to eat.

My mother struggled to bring up her seven children, as well as grieving for the ones that didn't survive. As a small child I recall her as permanently pregnant and suffering chronically from morning sickness. But what I most remember was my mother's confusing approach to discipline. It seemed that whenever any of my brothers had earned a punishment, my mother would take it out on one of her daughters instead. This seemed extremely unfair, so I decided to approach my mother to ask her why we were beaten for our brothers' misdemeanours. Patiently, she explained that boys may be physically stronger than girls but that their hearts are much more fragile, especially when admonished by a woman: a mother or lover. It was preferable, she said, that they learned to feel sorry for their sisters' suffering on their behalf. Consequently, of course, we became eager to discipline them ourselves, to prevent us earning any more beatings. But our mother also understood that one day her girls would become mistresses of home and husband. Eventually I came to realise that my mother had taught me a valuable lesson in understanding and managing my relationships with the opposite sex.

But life was not all discipline; we had many times that I remember with great fondness. On the coldest of winter evenings my father would erect a *korsi*: large woollen blankets were spread over the table in the centre of the living room, and a brazier containing hot charcoal was placed beneath it. It was here that we gathered for mealtimes, and it was here that we slept at night. I say we slept, but with all our mattresses gathered around this table and our feet warming close to the hot coals, we often chatted and laughed into the small hours.

During the summer vacations, there was a practice of children migrating to the mountains. This served several purposes, although ostensibly it was to escape the heat of the city. I don't doubt, however, that as well as providing a variety of experiences, it also gave our parents a break from the intensity of family life. Fully chaperoned, we stayed for several weeks in the local governor's house, not far from the famous mountain fortress of Alamut. It was here that my father's family traced its origins from centuries earlier.

I never met my paternal grandfather, but I learned that he had been the leader of our tribe; he was killed in a tribal war when my father was just seven years old.

The heads of the tribes of the Valleys of the Assassins near Alamut (circa 1910). Mahin's grandfather is second from right, holding a sword.

The journey to the mountains was an adventure in itself. There were no paved roads at the time, so we travelled along the dusty mountain tracks by mule. This exodus took three days and necessitated stopping over each night in local villages. We were always welcomed, and the heads of these villages were proud to act as our hosts. The highlight of these occasions was the entertaining stories they regaled us with after dinner. It was on nights such as this that we learned of many tales handed down the generations from the times of our ancestors.

One of the many stories recounted was how Hasan-i-Sabah captured a local fortress:

He approached the local tribespeople declaring his interest in purchasing some land. The usual practice for measuring land in those days was to measure it in areas equivalent to the surface area of the hide of an animal. When they asked him how many hides he wanted to buy and he replied, 'Just one,' they thought he was crazy and, pointing towards the mountains, invited him to help himself. Hasan proceeded to cut an animal hide into thin strips and knot them together before carefully placing his ribbon of skins around the nearest mountain, which he declared to be his own. The villagers laughed at him. Sometime later they discovered his plan to build a fortress and begin his struggles against the mighty Seljuk Empire.

I loved to listen to stories, and this practice was not restricted to the summer months. Once a week in wintertime a storyteller nicknamed Scheherazade would call in to tell us children a bedtime story from the tales of the *Thousand and One Nights*. Of course, the real Scheherazade was a Persian girl who saved her own life by keeping the caliph waiting until her next visit to hear the end of each story. Eventually he became so enthralled that he made her his wife. By breaking off the narrative when it was getting really exciting, our Scheherazade kept us children waiting in the same manner as her namesake.

Then there was gossip – lots of it – mostly the insidious kind that permeates all close-knit societies. Any girl caught in the act of passing more than the most cursory glance at any boy would give rise to a scandal. Worse still were the visitations! The seemingly endless arrival of parents eager to introduce their unmarried sons to my father. My sisters and I were widely regarded as pretty, and these hopeful parents were eager for a pledge of marriage. We disliked this parade intensely. I had always made it known that I would never marry a Ghazvinian boy, no matter how many times my father allowed these unwelcome guests into our home. Yet despite this, my father insisted that he had to respect local customs. We, therefore, had little choice but to resort to drastic action. One of my sisters climbed to the top of the walnut tree in the garden and refused to come down until the visitors departed, whilst I attempted something more subtle. In order to discourage some of the most despised ascetic families from trying their luck, I allowed a little gossip to spread, suggesting that my father drank alcohol.

My childhood years appeared to pass swiftly, but I had been happy and had certainly enjoyed my education. However, there were no secondary schools for girls in Ghazvin in those days, so my father hired private tutors to ensure his daughters continued to learn beyond the age of 11.

I particularly loved history and was captivated as I learned of the Achaemenid Empire and the exploits of our ancient kings Cyrus and Darius. In those days, women were honoured and revered and often held important and influential positions of state. Gender was not as restrictive as it was for us: both men and women enjoyed equal pay and equal rights. Women enlisted in the armed forces and, much to the consternation of our Roman and Greek enemies, often held high office. Cyrus the Great was the author of the world's first declaration of human rights – itself largely based on the liberal and progressive principles of the state religion, Zoroastrianism.

There was one lesson that I would never forget. My tutor was visibly emotional as he recounted the most catastrophic event in all of Persian history: the seventh-century Arab invasion and the imposition of Islam by force on the population. This invasion led to the destruction of our ancient civilisation and plunged our country into permanent darkness. I am aware that many disagree, but it is those dreadful events that largely explain the paradox of modern-day Iran: a society entirely divided between the believers in Islam and the many like me who cannot accept what Islam has done to our wonderful country.

Yet this is the country and society in which I was raised. I grew up to resent the extraneous influence of the Islamic aspects of Iranian culture. I resented the tradition of arranged marriages. I resented the Islamic teaching that a woman's opinion was considered to be worth only half that of a man's. Surely this is just insulting and utterly misogynistic? What on earth entered the Prophet's head that such an illogical and offensive edict should come to be recorded in the Koran? Even if not mandatory in those days, I resented that only women were expected to wear the veil. If a woman could be beautiful in a man's eyes, could not a man be equally handsome in a woman's eyes?

I became more inflamed by the idea of sexual injustice, even within my own family. Was it fair that my brothers were sent abroad to university, and I was not? I vowed to use all my strength to resist all that Islam imposed on our society. But I needed to be careful. It was vital to protect myself by being extremely discreet with my opinions, to never reveal personal information or private thoughts. It was at this age I began to develop an outer shell to disguise my revolutionary soul. My true inner self would only be revealed to someone I loved and trusted fully.

Women in Ghazvin wearing Western-style hats after Reza Shah issued a decree banning Islamic veils on January 8, 1936

At the same time as this protective shell was developing, so was my awareness of my effect on men. I had always been told I was beautiful, but now I could see for myself how men behaved around me, and I realised this placed me in a position of considerable power. I vowed to ensure I used these blessings to my own advantage. I know that may sound vain, but in many ways, I regarded it like holding an impressive hand in poker and knowing how to exploit it to win. In short, I became a *fighter*.

I learned to care little about what other people thought of me. Why should it matter? I had an acute ability to read people quickly. I determined to respect only those who earned my respect, and I naturally despised those who did not. If this made me a divisive figure, I was unconcerned.

In light of all my beliefs, it may have seemed paradoxical that I had so much admiration for my ancestor, Hasan-i-Sabah. But that is easy to explain. I understood that his devout reputation was a charade and that in reality he never believed a word of his own religious preaching. During his lifetime, he was first and foremost a patriot. Hasan exploited the Sunni/Shia schism in Islam purely for the political purposes of defending our nation against the occupying Seljuk Turks. Little did I appreciate it then, but over the centuries, this same schism would be used by the clergy in the form of a theocratic justification for political ends. My compatriots sometimes refer to this as a *sword* that when unsheathed is known as our *Shia Weapon*.

And as my beliefs strengthened, I became determined to influence my own future, and it was necessary to begin at home! With four growing daughters, life in the house became a constant battle for my father. We were all determined to pursue careers, and in the suffocating environment of Ghazvin that was simply not possible. After many arguments and attempts at persuasion, we finally succeeded in getting him to sell up in Ghazvin and move to Tehran. I was excited; new possibilities were now opening up for me.

2

A LESSON IN LOVE

The Moving Finger writes; and, having writ,
Moves on: nor all thy Piety nor Wit
Shall lure it back to cancel half a Line,
Nor all thy Tears wash out a Word of it.

Omar Khayyam

England 1956
John:

I knew from an early age that my parents planned for me to complete my secondary education in one of England's prestigious public schools. They chose to send me and my younger brother to Lancing College in Sussex, a school distinguished for having the largest school chapel in the world. It was our mother, a physiotherapist, who, having witnessed the awful consequences of spinal injuries inflicted on boys playing rugger, persuaded my father that her sons should attend a soccer school. Moreover, she was a staunch supporter of the Church of England,

and she particularly admired the intentions of Lancing's Founder, Nathaniel Woodward, in his plea for the middle classes, that religious education in his schools should be based on 'sound principle and sound knowledge, firmly grounded in the Catholic faith as expressed in the English *Book of Common Prayer*'. A Lancing education, she optimistically insisted, would equip her sons with an effortless superiority in all matters theological and evangelical.

Several months before I was due to begin, my mother took me shopping at Harrods to kit me out. Back at home, I gazed upon my transformed appearance in the bedroom mirror. I hardly recognised myself. Smirking with a mixture of embarrassment and pride, I caught the eye of my mother standing behind me.

'Quite a handsome young man already.' Her voice was affectionate and proud.

'Tall, blond hair and blue eyes… although the way these golden locks are growing, you'll soon need a haircut.'

I looked at her through the mirror.

'But you never wanted me to get my hair cut. You said you like it longer. Have you changed your mind?'

My mother looked wistful and took a minute to reply.

'Sooner or later those golden locks of hair and bright blue eyes will surely lead you into trouble, my boy. One day some wretch of a girl will steal my son from me.'

I was horrified to hear this and wanted to reassure her.

'Mummy, why would you say that? That's an awful idea.' I shuddered at the thought. 'And anyway, I'm only 13!'

But things had to change. I certainly had to have a haircut, and then I had to embark on my new school life as a boarder. It was the beginning of growing up.

I settled in well, but – academically speaking – I was by no means outstanding. It was with some trepidation that I returned home at the end of my first term and handed my father a sealed envelope. The dreaded first school report!

'Bottom of the bottom class in French!' my father bellowed in disbelief. His disappointment was evident.

'Well,' I replied somewhat arrogantly, 'inevitably someone must hold that distinction, and it just happens to be me.'

My father was not amused and clearly wanted a solution. 'I learnt French from a native speaker,' he said. 'He was a hopeless teacher, but he didn't speak a word of English. That's how I learned the language. I stopped thinking in English and began to think in French.'

I watched him as he thought for a few minutes. Suddenly he appeared inspired:

'I'll do the same for you, my boy. I'm sending you to France!'

***

France
Summer 1957 and 1958

The following year I spent three weeks on exchange staying with a huge family in a large chateau just south of Paris. The experience made a lasting impression, and it transformed me into something of a Francophile. On returning home from school a year later, I handed my report to my father with a huge smile on my face.

'Top of the class above in French, then. Aren't you going to thank me for having sent you to France?'

'Yes, Daddy, it was a brilliant idea. In fact, I've planned to go to another family living in the South of France. And I'm going to study German as well.'

'Excellent, and go to Germany?'

'Yes, but not before my third year in school.'

'Where in France will you be going?'

'I've arranged an exchange through school: the Pays Basque. And this time I'm travelling by train.'

'Sounds like fun. But don't do anything I wouldn't!'

For this exchange I had been allocated a partner named Francis. He was waiting to greet me as I arrived, and he was accompanied by his mother and two younger sisters. In contrast to the previous year, there was no chateau; instead they showed me round their villa, situated in a large garden. This was a marvellous part of France, with a fantastic climate. The house was just a short drive from the very fashionable seaside resort of Biarritz, and with just six people around the table for meals, this was very much a family affair and far more intimate.

I was maturing in other ways too. I was very attracted to the new wave of Italian movie stars: Sophia Loren, Claudia Cardinale and Gina Lollobrigida. I was quite enthralled by these dark-haired beauties. Maybe it was because I was so fair myself. Imagine how exciting it was to discover that Francis's mother, with her black hair and dark brown eyes, bore a very strong resemblance to these idols. Before long I was instinctively taking every opportunity to steal glances at my hostess.

It was just a matter of time before she noticed, and my behaviour, however discreet, inevitably provoked a reaction. She was a talented cook, and noticing how much I enjoyed her food and how frequently I complimented her on her culinary skills, she seemed to make a special effort with her appearance at dinner. One Sunday she produced a wonderful lunch of roast lamb, garnished not with the customary mint sauce I was used to – but with garlic.

'There you are,' she said, placing the joint on the table in front of her husband as she handed him the carving knife and fork.

The children watched their father attentively. Realising that his attention, as well as her children's, was focused on the task in hand, she remained standing just behind him, looking and smiling directly at me. As I looked at her, I noted she had taken extra care with her make-up that morning. Her dark brown eyes were perfectly accentuated with black liner and mascara, her red lipstick was freshly applied and through her jet-black hair she had tied a red ribbon. Her appearance was stunning, and for several perfect seconds, she held me in her gaze. I looked straight into her eyes and vainly tried to prevent myself from blushing. I realised that she knew exactly what she was doing and that she was relishing every moment of it. Was she being deliberately cruel? Even if I was physically mature for my age, I was an inexperienced 15-year-old lad, and she was a married woman more than twice my age. Yet I was lost – as far as I was concerned, I might have been staring at Sophia Loren. Reluctantly I forced my gaze away from her; I was in danger of losing all self-control. In that moment, I would have done anything for her.

The following day Francis decided that we children should play Monopoly and that he would be banker. This game went on for hours, with Francis bending the rules to make sure no one went bankrupt. By the early afternoon I had had enough and refused to be bailed out by Francis's bank for the umpteenth time. At that minute his mother came into the room.

'I'm going shopping. Is anyone coming with me?'

I jumped at the opportunity. '*Je viendrais avec vous!*'

We drove to a supermarket on the outskirts of Bayonne, and as soon as *Madame* (I only ever called her '*Madame*') had finished her shopping and put it in the car, she suggested that we go for a walk in a nearby park.

Walking in the shade of the trees in the hot afternoon sun was quite delightful. The park was almost deserted, and as we disappeared through a shady glade, well obscured from prying eyes, I desperately wanted to hold her hand. Obviously I dared not suggest this, so we walked on apart. Eventually we came to a grassy bank and lay down side by side.

For a few moments we lay there in silence.

'Married life is just so hard.'

I was shocked and at a loss for a reply.

Then she did exactly what I had dared not do: she took my hand in hers and turned to look at me.

'*Les chaines, John, les chaines* – I have to do everything for my children, I have to!' Holding my hand still tighter she lay looking up at the sky while I rolled towards her, staring into her eyes and listening to her words. I didn't understand everything she said, but it was enough to listen to her voice and just to look at her. After a while she paused and stared straight at me. Her heavy scent filled my senses, and she smiled. I bent down a little closer, and understanding immediately what my intention was, she put her hands around my neck and pulled my lips down on hers. In my few years on earth, I had never experienced anything like this. I was being kissed by a truly beautiful woman. For a minute or two we gazed at one another. My entire body was tense, flooded by the ecstasy of our closeness. She brushed her fingers through my hair, and I wondered if it was my blond hair, so different from hers, that had attracted her. This moment was so exquisite that tears filled my eyes and began to trickle onto my cheeks. Gently, she touched them as they fell, and equally gently she wiped them away.

We kissed again, even more passionately, until quite abruptly, she pushed me away. 'I'm sorry, I shouldn't have encouraged you, it's all my fault.'

'Why? I've never been so happy in my life.' She tried to sit up but I was holding her and trying desperately to extend our beautiful moment. Rolling from my grasp, she raised herself up and adjusted her clothing.

'This would end badly. You're just 15 years old, and I'm a married woman. It's absolutely ridiculous!'

She stood up and indicated that I should follow her. We walked back to the car in silence. I searched in vain for the right thing to say, but I was lost in confusion. Once seated in the car, she found a tissue in her handbag and swiftly wiped her lipstick off my lips and face – the same lips and face that she had, only minutes ago, wiped so gently with those fingers. After checking that no evidence remained, she put the key in the ignition and drove home.

On our arrival Francis came to greet us. He was babbling enthusiastically about having beaten his sisters at Monopoly.

'It was fun. You missed it all!'

If only he knew …

For the rest of my stay my hostess refrained from looking at me, and she no longer put a red ribbon in her hair. But the deed had been done; she had stolen my heart. I had great difficulty in accepting the fact that my affection for her had no future, and at that age I believed I could never love anyone else. Did she know what she had done to me? Was it a game: a light relief from stressful family life? Or had she really felt something for me and been carried away by that moment? One thing was certain – I had learned more than just French that summer.

3

THE ACCIDENT

As far as you can avoid it, do not give grief to anyone.
Never inflict your rage on another.
If you hope for eternal rest, feel the pain yourself, but don't hurt others.

Omar Khayyam

Mahin:

My childhood dream had been to study medicine and to one day become a surgeon. But if opportunities for ambitious girls were scarce in my hometown, it didn't appear that different in Tehran. So, on completion of my secondary education, I pursued a course in modern languages and literature at university, and it was during this time that I managed to secure a position as secretary to the minister of agriculture. I became one of the many students in those days who worked in offices until two in the afternoon and then spent the late afternoon and evening attending classes.

But our home life in Tehran was different to our life in Ghazvin, and with the exception of my elder brothers who were studying abroad, we all lived together in a large apartment in the city centre. My younger brother Fereydoon inhabited the bedroom next to mine. I say 'inhabited' because he lived an almost independent life from the rest of us, getting out of bed at lunchtime and going back to bed just before dawn. We rarely encountered him except at mealtimes. That much was tolerable, but he was a lead violinist in the Tehran Symphony Orchestra and insisted on practising his violin nightly and well into the small hours. Living with my family was gradually becoming a nightmare.

Early one morning, a few months following the visit to the fortune teller, I awoke with a piercing headache. It had been another night of Fereydoon's nocturnal torturing of his violin. What a bad start to such an important day. Today, my minister was expecting a visit from his opposite number in Romania. The whole ministry would be on show. Obviously, this meant that I had to look the part. I had no intention of letting my boss down as he had gone to great lengths to hire me. Having been tipped off by a colleague about my talents, he had travelled all the way to Ghazvin, where I was working in a regional office, to interview me. I was well aware that my beauty was part of the reason I got the job.

Seated at my dressing table, I applied make-up with even more care than usual. And once I was satisfied with my face, I moved to the wardrobe to select my most flattering and professional outfit: a white blouse and fitted black skirt. Finally, I added red shoes and a tight-fitting red leather belt to accentuate my hips. Pleasing my boss was important, but that was as nothing compared to pleasing – or rather teasing – the Romanian minister himself. The trick was to do it in such manner as to deny him even the slightest opportunity of familiarity.

There was just time for one last appraisal in the mirror before my driver pulled up outside the gate. I picked up my red handbag and the small black briefcase containing my university work and descended the stairs. As I walked across the front garden, my driver was standing and holding the car door. Moments later we were gliding along the streets of Tehran on our way to the ministry.

'Is there something special on at the ministry today, Miss Rashvand?' Abbas asked, barely taking his eyes off the mirror.

'Why do you ask, Abbas?'

'Madam is beautifully dressed today. I can't help wondering if there is a special reason.'

'You see me every morning. Am I not always beautifully dressed, Abbas?'

'Madam, of course you are. It's just that today you look more splendid than usual.'

'You're very observant, Abbas. Well, as a matter of fact, you're right. We're expecting a ministerial delegation from Romania.'

A few minutes later we pulled up in front of the ministry. Abbas quickly jumped out and opened my door. I climbed the steps and walked straight through the entrance to where a porter was standing by one of the lifts.

I glanced at him anxiously. 'Has the minister arrived yet?'

'Not yet, ma'am.'

I always made a point of getting in before him, but on this important day he may have arrived earlier than usual. On reaching the top floor, I went straight into his office to check it was suitably tidy. A large bunch of fresh flowers stood in an elegant vase beside his expansive desk, and yes, the daily newspaper was in its usual place.

A few minutes later I heard the lift doors open, and the minister, a former army general, quite literally marched in. Before I could greet him, he began issuing orders. 'Miss Rashvand, please ask all my assistants to come to my office immediately and provide us all with copies of today's agenda for the 10 o'clock meeting. You'll recollect, Miss Rashvand, that the Romanians are happy to sell us their produce in exchange for hard currency, but when they buy from us, they always want to pay in kind. It gets very complicated! I want to run through the details before negotiations begin in earnest.'

I returned to my desk and asked one of my colleagues to place copies of the agenda on the meeting table in the minister's office while I began calling his assistants.

At 10 o'clock exactly, the call came from ground-floor reception to advise that the Romanian delegation had arrived. I went straight into the minister's office to inform him. 'Show them into the conference room, please, Miss Rashvand, and we'll join them shortly.'

I went to the lobby to greet the guests. As the Romanian minister emerged from the lift, he walked straight towards me. I offered him my hand, which he kissed in a distinctly ceremonious manner.

'What a pleasure – such a charming reception. Surely the world's most beautiful women are to be found in this land.' I smiled, acknowledging the compliment, and immediately turned to lead his delegation into the conference room. His party of five, having taken their places, rose as soon as the Iranian minister entered with his assistants. I stood and watched as the introductions were made.

'I do hope that your charming secretary will remain with us – at least to take the minutes,' the Romanian minister suggested optimistically. 'I'm sure she will keep us all wide awake and fully attentive.'

My boss smiled. 'Ah yes, I remember your visit last year. I was definitely of the impression that you'd come more to see my secretary than to see me.'

Fortunately, I was spared by the arrival of the office boy bearing tea. I quickly took my leave.

However, if I had imagined that was to be the most eventful part of my day, I was wrong. Later that morning, I received a call from Tahira. 'Have you heard the news?'

'What news?'

'Azar is in hospital!'

'Whatever for?'

'She's had a terrible car accident.'

I let that thought sink in for a moment whilst Tahira continued babbling.

'Mahin, when people in the street pulled her from the tangled wreck of her car, they thought she'd gone mad.'

'Mad? Why mad?'

'She kept repeating the words "thank God, thank God". You know what that means, don't you?'

I didn't want to think about it. I kept imagining the state that Azar must be in.

'Which hospital is she in?'

'I don't know yet. When I find out, I'll call you back so that we can arrange to go and visit her.'

'Yes, please do. See you later.' The line went dead. For several minutes I sat looking at the wall opposite my desk, reflecting on what I had heard. It was exactly as the fortune teller had predicted for her; it was uncanny. How could she have foretold something like this? Although I had enjoyed my particular reading, I had been very sceptical of the whole thing. Now my belief was wavering…

The following day Tahira and I bought some flowers and went to visit Azar in hospital. She had been thrown through the car windscreen, and only her eyes and mouth were visible beneath the bandages. Tahira looked like she might cry.

'So, the fortune teller was right after all.'

Azar nodded.

'But now you're released.'

Azar nodded again, unable to speak.

'How bad is it… under those, I mean?' I indicated the bandages on her face.

Azar shook her head and muttered something inaudible. The nurse answered for her.

'She's going to be all right, but she'll need a lot of plastic surgery.'

Tahira made a small whimpering sound and the nurse looked at her kindly, assuming her concerns to be all for her friend. I wondered, however, if in that moment she had a glimpse of what her own prediction would bring.

In the weeks that followed Tahira and I visited Azar almost daily while the surgeons did their work. A few months later, although her wounds had almost entirely healed, some scars remained as a permanent reminder.

It wasn't long before something else occurred to underscore the fortune teller's premonitions. I was having breakfast with my parents when my father announced he had something to say. He began by addressing me as his wisest and most sensible daughter, something that pleased me immeasurably; then he went on to say that he had been discussing my future with my mother.

'Now that the family estates have been sold off in Ghazvin and my business successfully re-established here in Tehran, we've decided that we should move out of this apartment into a smaller one.'

I looked at him with concern. A smaller apartment? I already found it difficult enough to study and sleep, with Fereydoon and his violin!

He smiled, noting my worried face.

'We realise that this is not very convenient for you, with your work at the ministry and your studies at university. So, with your agreement, I'm prepared to offer you the money to buy yourself a house near here.'

I was incredulous; it was a dream come true.

'I should also mention that your cousin Roshan and her husband, Hooshang, who, as you know, have a child now, are looking for somewhere to rent hereabouts. It would be ideal if you could find a two-storey house where you could live upstairs and rent downstairs to them. This solves the problem of chaperones as, together, you would constitute a perfectly respectable household.

I leapt to my feet and threw my arms around my father's neck and kissed the top of his head. 'What a wonderful father you are. That's absolutely marvellous.'

'Mahin, you must promise me, on your word of honour, that you'll never bring any strange men alone into your house.'

'I promise, Father, never.'

A few weeks later Roshan and I succeeded in finding a suitable two-storey house close to Aryamehr Avenue and just a short distance from the ministry. As it was customary in Iran to pay for houses in cash, I arranged to meet my father at his bank, taking my brother-in-law Heshmatollah, a police colonel, and Roshan's husband, Hooshang, an army colonel, along for protection. We then went to the offices of a notary public to complete the transaction. The cash was placed on the notary's desk, and he watched as it was counted first by the seller and then by the buyer before being signed for. The notary then invited the seller and myself to sign the transfer deed. I picked up the pen, but quite unexpectedly my hand trembled, and the pen fell to the floor.

'What's the matter?' the notary asked in astonishment, as I bent down to pick the pen up.

'I'm sorry. Please excuse me. I'm a little nervous. Something just occurred to me.'

'What is it?'

I paused to catch my breath. I couldn't possibly explain.

'Nothing, really, it's just the excitement of something coming into my name.'

The notary shrugged, and the rest of the transaction was executed without flaw.

Early the following day I received a call from a long-standing family acquaintance, General Jahanbani. Iranian society in those days was undergoing massive social and structural change as part of what the shah called his 'White Revolution'. It was named 'white' as opposed to 'red' since it was intended to be bloodless. A major aspect of that so-called revolution was land reform. This reform involved breaking up the great estates hitherto owned by what were known as the 'Thousand Families' and redistributing the land to the peasants. It was a controversial policy that not only upset the aristocracy but more significantly the clergy, who had seen their stipends dramatically cut back by the shah's father. They were now forced to depend on their estates for a large part of their income. General Jahanbani had one such family as he still owned extensive estates in northern Iran. He never missed a chance to take advantage of whatever the Ministry of Agriculture could provide by way of support, and he knew that the quickest way to access the minister to discuss his needs was through me.

'Good morning, General,' I began. 'I'm afraid the minister is away. He's travelling and won't be back in his office until next week.'

'Well, maybe you can help me. You know that I've some large estates in Mazandaran. We're looking for all kinds of assistance with fertilizers, seeds, imported farm machinery and so forth, and I would really like to come to your office and discuss it with the minister.'

'No problem, General. If you don't want to wait until the minister returns, I can put you through to one of his assistants. Please hold the line a minute… There you are, you're through now.'

A few minutes later my phone rang again. It was Azar.

'Mahin, I've heard that you've been house hunting.'

'Who told you that?'

'Never mind. Have you found anything?'

'Well, actually, yes, I've just bought a house near Avenue Aryamehr.'

'Lucky you: a wonderful job and now a house. Some people get all the luck! But why all the secrecy? And you were the one who insisted that nothing the fortune teller said would ever come true. Now what do you think? Are you elated or shocked?'

'Certainly shocked: my hand was trembling so much that I dropped the pen in the notary's office just before I signed the deed. He wondered what was wrong with me. But of course, I'm very happy.'

'All you need now is a young man with blond hair and blue eyes to share it with.'

She giggled and I laughed along with her, but I couldn't admit to thinking something similar.

'When's the house-warming party? I definitely want an invitation.'

'It's not planned yet, but yes, of course you'll get an invite – along with that black-eyed, black-haired husband of yours.'

'I doubt you'll get around to it before you're holding a wedding reception!'

'Cheeky! That's enough. I must get on. Bye for now, Azar.' And I hung up, but throughout that day, I confess, my mind was not entirely on my work.

4

THE SHAH'S GIFT TO HIS PEOPLE

Drink wine and look at the moon
And think of all the civilisations
The moon has seen passing by.

Omar Khayyam

England
Spring 1969
John:

On leaving school in 1960, I decided to follow a career in
the construction industry, and pursuant to my studies at
Regent Street Polytechnic, I worked for several years in
various professional offices in London. By the spring of
1969 I had taken my final examination, and I was confident
that I would qualify as a chartered surveyor. I was 26 years
old, and like many young men my age, I sought to broaden
my horizons. With this intention, I began looking for a job
on the other side of the English Channel. I was fortunate to
be offered a position in a new office in Zurich as assistant

to the general manager. Taking possession of a new car, I drove across France and on arrival in Zurich checked into a hotel to rendezvous with my colleague, who had arrived a few days earlier.

The weeks that followed were spent looking for offices and rental accommodation. By the beginning of May the office was furnished, but hardly had we started work when I received a telephone call from a senior partner at Head Office in London to enquire whether I could be spared for six to eight weeks for a job in Tehran. The office manager and I stared at one another in complete astonishment. 'In Tehran? Where's that? Iran, Persia? The Middle East?'

As I was already committed to act as best man at my brother's wedding the following weekend, it was agreed that I would fly out the day after the ceremony. I was to be accompanied on the trip by Harry Eastwood, one of the senior partners from London.

The day after the wedding was Sunday 11th May. It was with some trepidation that I set about packing my bags. What should I take with me? I was unfamiliar with my destination, but I did know that Tehran was located four thousand feet above sea level: which was about equal to the top of Ben Nevis. Would it be cold, snowy even, or hot and tropical? Was it possible to go skiing? As time was short, I stuffed a variety of garments into my suitcase. By the time my father dropped me off at Heathrow Airport, an impatient Harry was already waiting for me.

'We're on Iran Air,' he grumbled. 'It's a round trip of Europe: Paris, then Frankfurt, Istanbul and Tehran. Had it not been for that bloomin' wedding of yours, we could've left days ago on a direct flight with British Airways.'

'What time do we arrive in Tehran, then?' I asked.

'Five o'clock in the bloomin' morning!'

Immediately after take-off, Harry reached for the button above his seat, and an air hostess arrived.

'Two vodka limes please! When's lunch?'

'Dinner will be served after Frankfurt.'

'I'm starving! Please bring some pistachio nuts.' Harry, turning towards me, continued, 'I realise that this is your first trip to Iran, but actually they do have some quite nice things there, and one of them is a drink known as vodka lime, made from Iranian vodka, lime juice, 7up and, of course, ice. Another is pistachio nuts, and they do go very well together.'

'Cheers!'

'Something they don't have in Iran is waitresses, but you may have noticed that Iran Air does in fact have air hostesses. At 30 thousand feet, *houris* in paradise, so to speak.'

'I had noticed,' I replied, 'and judging by the looks of them, the shah might just have hand-picked them himself.'

'Now there's a thought – you might be right.'

A few minutes later Harry's glass was empty, and once again he stretched his hand up to the call button above his head. The air hostess came back down the gangway. Harry held up his empty glass and politely raised two fingers indicating that he would like two more vodka limes.

Just as he was about to order a third round of drinks, the fasten seat belt signs illuminated, and the pilot announced that our landing in Paris was imminent. I thought I had better ask some questions.

'Where will we be staying in Tehran?'

'Our services are provided to the project as part of a package deal together with the services of the structural engineers. They've rented a large villa in downtown Tehran with numerous rooms. It's quite comfortable, and we'll have a room each with shared bathroom facilities.'

It all sounded acceptable. I settled back for the second leg of the journey. And not long after take-off from Paris, the pilot announced that we were about to land in Frankfurt.

'I really don't care much for French beer, but German beer is quite another matter,' Harry said as the landing gear went down for a second time.

'How long will you be staying in Tehran?' I asked.

'We're arriving Monday and I plan to leave on Thursday, which should be long enough to arrange introductions and explain what you'll be doing for the next few weeks. Thursday is like Saturday in Europe, the end of the week in Iran, and there will be little point in me hanging around any longer.'

Some minutes later the plane touched down, and we stepped into the transit lounge to sample the local beer. Back on board, Harry ordered yet another round of vodka limes. 'It really is a very refreshing drink with no apparent after-effects,' I mused, 'but sooner or later it'll catch up with us, surely?'

Before Harry could reply, an air hostess arrived with our meal of grilled chicken and rice with vegetables. But I didn't look at the food, as I was fascinated by the hostess leaning across Harry towards me. She had beautiful black hair, black eyes and the tiniest waist. I certainly hadn't seen any women this attractive in Switzerland. I was becoming just a little bit excited about the prospect of this trip.

Of course, I had had relationships – even intimate ones – with several girls, all of them English, since leaving school almost 10 years earlier, but visually speaking in my eyes at least, none of them were comparable with this young lady. I recalled two girls who had successfully plucked at my heart strings before ditching me. I shuddered to think what that experience might have been like had I fallen for a beautiful Iranian girl like this one.

Harry, however, was more concerned about filling his stomach and over dinner explained that in Iran there was a wide choice of delicious fruit and vegetables as well as many varieties of nuts. 'The cuisine is different from anything we know in Europe and on occasion, quite exotic.'

'Like the girls, you mean?'

'Good heavens, John, we haven't even arrived yet. Aren't you hungry? I'm beginning to wonder whether sending you to Iran was such a good idea after all.'

Harry finished his wine and tucked into the dessert. 'Perhaps I should tell you a bit more about the project,' he began. 'It's huge and far more than just another office building. The footprint is equivalent in area to at least two football pitches end to end. The structure rises vertically through some 15 storeys up to what is referred to as the podium level. From that point upwards, it divides into two narrower sections, each about 18 metres wide, facing east and west, that then rise from the podium through another 20 storeys. So far so good, but these two narrower upper sections each lean outward and away from each other to such an extent that their respective centres of gravity extend beyond their toppling point.'

Harry raised his arms in the air and stretched them wide apart to illustrate what he was trying to explain.

'You mean it's a bit like the Eiffel Tower stood upside down?'

'You're beginning to get the idea. It'll be clearer when you see the drawings tomorrow.'

'And what about the lifts? Do they go up sideways like those in the lower sections of the Eiffel Tower?'

'Good question. Well actually, no, they don't. The lifts are grouped in four stand-alone vertical tower structures that rise from ground level up to the top, two on the east and two on the west elevations respectively, spaced equidistantly along each elevation. And that's not all – the whole bloomin' thing has to be earthquake proof. Can you imagine?'

Harry produced a pen from his briefcase and was busy sketching on his paper napkin.

'As you'll see tomorrow, the British structural engineers are hard at work designing and calculating a structural steel frame.'

'One hell of a lot of steel,' I said. 'Are our fees based on a percentage of the weight?'

'We are not that fortunate!'

'Who on earth came up with such a crazy idea to construct an office building like that?'

'Another good question. You may be surprised to learn that the answer has a great deal to do with female anatomy.'

'Female anatomy? You're joking?'

'You might think so, but no,' Harry went on. 'You see, the architects for this project are Iranian. One should certainly not underrate them. They were busy building their famous city of Persepolis some 2,500 years ago when we Brits were not much beyond constructing Stonehenge. That's why they don't take kindly to any remarks suggesting they don't know what they're doing. The architects actually won this job in an architectural competition.' Harry paused a moment.

'Yes, yes,' I said, 'but what's all this got to do with female anatomy?'

'Aha, well, you see, the story goes that the younger of the two architects paid a visit one evening to a Tehran nightclub – there are quite a few in the city – and the girls began turning cartwheels on the stage. Then quite suddenly one of them with exceptionally long, elegant legs did a handstand. At first, she appeared motionless, and then slowly, very slowly, she parted her legs into a great "V" and for a few seconds held them there before bringing them back together again. The young architect, who for some time had been searching for an inspiration, immediately visualised his design and, seized by enthusiasm, rushed back to his office in the middle of the night and drew the office block I've just described.'

'You're joking!'

'Well, I wasn't there with him in the nightclub, but the story has never been denied.'

'That's just unbelievable. Is that how he won the competition?'

'Another good question,' Harry replied. 'Probably, yes. The fact is that the shah himself adjudicated the various proposals and took his wife the empress Farah along with him. Now the empress, before she met her husband, had been a student of architecture in Paris. Unsurprisingly, therefore, she was invited to make the final choice. And, apparently, she was utterly amazed at this daring and futuristic design, so the contract was awarded.

'Goodness! And did the young architect explain the origin of the inspiration?'

'John,' Harry said, reaching for the button above his head again, 'you're making me thirsty.'

A few moments later the air hostess reappeared.

'What would you like, sir?'

'Two more vodka limes, please.' Harry turned his gaze towards me. 'I think you're letting your sense of humour get in the way of your sense of judgement.'

'A few more vodka limes and I doubt I will have any sense of judgement at all.'

'To continue, the fact is the shah formally declared at a press conference that this project would become "his gift to the Iranian people".'

'That was a bit of a supercilious idea, wasn't it?'

'Never mind whether it was or whether it wasn't. I should remind you that tomorrow we shall be landing in Tehran, the capital city of the Empire of Iran. We don't comment on Iranian politics, at least not if we want to work there.'

'The Empire of Iran?'

'Yes, that's what they call the country.'

'Yes, but it used to be called Persia years ago. Why was the name changed?'

The hostess returned with the vodka limes.

'My understanding is that the present shah's father, Reza Shah, changed it for two reasons: firstly, because geographically Fars or Pars, to which the name Persia refers, is the name of a province and not the whole country, and secondly because he wanted the world to understand that Iran – in contrast to its neighbours – is the land of the Aryans and most specifically that the Iranic peoples are not Arabs or Turks but, being of Caucasian descent, more akin to Europeans. The present shah has gone even further and takes the title "*shah-an-shah Aryamehr*", which literally translated means "King of Kings and Light of the Aryans". It's true that the title "*shah-an-shah*" dates from at least the Achaemenid period, but the addition of "*Aryamehr*" seems to be something quite new.'

The seat belt signs switched back on again as the plane descended into Istanbul.

'You do realise that we're not even halfway yet.'

After Istanbul I slept through the final three-hour leg, only jolting awake as the plane landed in Tehran. It was pitch black outside, and oil lamps lined the fringes of the runway. By local time, it was half past five in the morning, and the small flames of the lamps looked quite magical.

Outside the airport terminal the first glimmer of dawn was just becoming visible. We clambered into an old orange Mercedes-Benz taxi. A few minutes after leaving the terminal the taxi pulled over, and another man sat in the front seat.

Somewhat surprised, I asked Harry who the man was.

'Another fare – a kamikaze,' Harry replied, laughing.

'I thought we had just landed in Iran, not Japan.'

'You'll find out shortly that we may have landed in hell. We haven't reached the city outskirts yet, and the population is mostly still asleep, but Tehran taxi drivers tend to drive in the middle of the road. Expats call the front seat the kamikaze seat! If a driver anticipates an accident, he doesn't brake – he accelerates. It's what's known as "the law of the bumper".'

I must have looked confused as he felt the need to elaborate.

'The vehicle that is further back in the direction of travel on impact is considered liable for any damages arising. See? It's better to accelerate before impact.' He laughed and continued in a whisper.

'Iranian drivers rarely look in their rear mirror – except to look at their passengers – any vehicle behind their own is considered irrelevant. In time, you'll get used to it – even if your nerves don't.'

'But what about the extra passenger?' I persisted.

'Maximising income: keep the taxi as full as possible, rather like a bus.'

I was captivated and confused in equal measure. I hardly dared look through the windows as it all appeared strangely chaotic.

A few moments later a pedestrian stepped out in front of the taxi on what appeared to be a pedestrian crossing.

Apart from honking his horn loudly in apparent protest, the taxi driver all but ignored the pedestrian, narrowly swerving around him on screeching tyres.

'But that's absolutely terrifying!'

'You'll get used to it,' Harry replied nonchalantly.

About half an hour later we pulled up outside a house in Shah Reza Avenue. Having no local currency, it took Harry a few minutes to persuade the taxi driver to accept a 20-dollar note. It took an even longer time to persuade someone in the house to open the front door.

Following a few introductions, we were grateful to fall into our beds.

On waking later that morning, one of the first things I noticed was the ambient temperature, already a contrast to our damp English climate. I wandered out of my room and discovered Harry scouring the villa to find breakfast. We both realised soon enough that there was no food. Even the refrigerator was bare.

'That's exactly what happens when a bunch of bachelors move in together.' Harry laughed. 'There's a sandwich shop 10 minutes' walk along the road near the office. We can get something there.'

The sun was high in the sky, its light and heat intense despite the altitude. To reach the shop we needed to get to the other side of the Shah Reza Avenue, which was four lanes wide in both directions. The traffic was so heavy, I feared we would never cross.

'There's only one way,' Harry shouted at the top of his voice, holding up his briefcase in his left hand in front of an oncoming car. 'They say that pedestrian crossings are painted white in this city to show up the colour of pedestrians' blood!'

We were halfway across now with taxis, cars and huge trucks grinding past in each direction just inches from where we stood. Harry moved his briefcase from his left hand to his right. There was a screeching of brakes and a screaming of horns as we hopped, skipped and jumped across another four lanes of traffic to the sidewalk on the opposite side of the road.

Shah Reza Avenue, in common with Tehran's wider avenues, is graced with mature plane trees that in summer provide welcome shelter from the scorching sun. These trees are huge and serve as a framing around the whole avenue. They are planted in jubes – or water channels – that divide the sidewalks from the main carriageways and are irrigated in this way. The source of this reliable supply of crystal-clear water is the melting snow of the Alborz Mountains. This range rises to around 14 thousand feet and stands over the north of the city like a great wall. By the end of summer only the very peaks of the mountains are covered in snow, but as autumn returns the snowline progressively creeps downwards. By December the entire city is engulfed once again.

We both stood still for a moment, absorbing our surroundings; then Harry resumed his role as my guide. 'Those peaks there are almost as high as Mont Blanc, but if you look further east, about 50 kilometres distant you can just see the summit of the dormant volcano, known as *Damavand*. That's more than 18 thousand feet and makes the Alborz the fourth highest mountain range in the world.'

But despite the spectacular scenery, we were still hungry, so we continued walking until we reached our shop. The glass cabinets on the counter displayed a tempting array of mini baguettes: ham and salami with gherkins, sliced eggs and tomatoes.

'This is an Armenian shop – being Christians they eat at least everything we do. Do you prefer Coke or 7up?'

Shortly afterwards, we walked down the side street, which provided a peaceful contrast to the main thoroughfare, and turned into the entrance hall of a modest-sized multi-storey office building. A doorman opened the lift door, and Harry pressed the button for the fifth floor. As the door opened into a large central hall, I was amazed by what confronted me. Encased in glass was a huge-scale model of the *shah-an-shah's* gift to his people: the proposed new headquarters building for the National Iranian Oil Company.

'Big enough?' Harry asked.

'It's absolutely massive – I suppose that's the model submitted for the architectural competition? I wonder how they ever carried it up the stairs.'

'More intelligent questions, John. As a matter of fact, there's a story about that too. It's said that, having initially drawn the project out on paper, the architects had to adjust its overall dimensions. They had to make it feasible to construct a model at an adequate scale that could be manoeuvred in and out of offices. Just imagine that.'

'Are you sure they didn't cut the model in half for that purpose?' I asked while carefully inspecting it for hairline cracks.

I was so engrossed in the structure that I hadn't noticed a receptionist in the hallway until she stood up to greet us. She then disappeared into an adjacent office before emerging again to welcome us in. The remainder of the day was spent in informal discussions with the Iranian architects and the British engineers.

Back at the villa that evening, there was still nothing to eat. One of the engineers volunteered to go shopping for eggs, bread, bacon and fresh vegetables for a fry-up.

'Don't much fancy that,' Harry remarked. 'I'd rather take you all out for dinner, but some of us are rather tired after a long flight, so it would have to be early. We need a proper night's sleep. Any suggestions?'

'What about the Chattanooga Restaurant up Pahlavi Avenue?' suggested an engineer. 'The food is really good, but there are five of us, so we'll need more than one taxi.'

'Ahhh yes – and there's a nightclub underneath that opens later.' Harry clearly knew this city.

'Well, we can leave that for another day,' the engineer replied.

'Famous last words.'

Soon all five of us were out on the street waving down taxis. As it happened, a large empty taxi came along, and we all managed to squeeze in, four in the back seat and me in the kamikaze seat. The rush hour was just coming to an end, and the traffic was starting to quicken. It was a terrifying journey. The driver honked his horn constantly as he wildly swerved the vehicle left to right. It appeared to be a national sport. My body was thrown around quite violently, and I dearly wished I had a seat belt.

'Are there no driving regulations in this country?' I enquired once I had reassembled myself on the sidewalk.

'Sure there are, but there's a common expression here: "*It's not Koran*", which effectively means that you can do anything you like provided it's not forbidden by the book. And to the best of my limited knowledge, the Koran contains no driving regulations!'

The Chattanooga Restaurant turned out to be a sophisticated establishment with a large floor area and numerous tables, apparently modelled on the Chattanooga Station building in Tennessee. Harry took charge by ordering five vodka limes, after which we were brought various salad dishes and then one of the most delicious courses that I have ever tasted: sturgeon kebab marinated in fresh lime juice and saffron. This fish, simply cooked on a charcoal grill, was a dish from paradise.

Ice cream followed, and at around 10 o'clock Harry asked for the bill. Some minutes later the waiter returned and handed it to an indignant Harry.

'What's this, 55 vodka limes?'

The waiter cast an eye over all of our party before addressing our spokesman.

'With all due respect, sir, unlike you and your distinguished guests, I can still count without losing my head.'

Harry raised an eyebrow and handed over his American Express card.

That night five rather drunken Englishmen staggered out of the restaurant and almost fell downstairs into the nightclub below. Once our eyes adjusted, we could see a cancan being performed on stage by a troupe of glamorous Lebanese girls. I found my eyes lingering on their long legs and I could feel my cheeks flush with mingled embarrassment and delight. One performance followed another. Suddenly there was a roll of drums, and the dancers began to cartwheel round in a large circle. When they finished this routine, a girl I had already noticed as having exceptionally long legs moved into the centre of the stage. I was captivated as she performed a handstand. Holding this precise position for several seconds, she then proceeded to open her legs exquisitely slowly. We were transfixed as we gazed at her wide-apart legs. In the seconds she was upside down, she appeared to be looking directly at Harry. In response, and quite impulsively, Harry began clapping, and as the rest of the audience joined in, he leaned over towards me and said, 'And there you have it!'

'You mean…'

'Yes, that's the handstand that's brought us all to Tehran and that has determined the principal characteristic of the building destined to be His Majesty's gift to his people.'

A little while later this long-legged Lebanese beauty came and sat down at our table. She clearly intended to speak to Harry.

'I couldn't help noticing that you were staring straight at me when I was doing my handstand. What was going through your mind? I hope it was nothing disrespectful.'

Harry chuckled as though he was about to choke, and a waiter immediately stepped forward and took an order for drinks. Harry regained his composure.

'How long have you been performing in this nightclub?'

'On and off for more than a year now. We're a travelling troupe, and we come over from Beirut every six weeks for a two-week visit.'

'Well, my dear,' Harry continued, 'I can assure you that my thoughts were in no way disrespectful. I was just contemplating what the skyline of this great city might look like in a few years' time and what the reaction of its population might be when its citizens see a replica of your wonderful legs on top of what will be its tallest building.'

She stared at Harry in disbelief. 'You mean someone is going to put a replica of my legs on top of the tallest building in Tehran? I don't believe it!'

'Not *your* legs, exactly,' Harry continued, 'but a building that will look like your legs performing a handstand.'

'Will they put my name on it?'

Harry roared. Placing a hand on hers, he declared, 'I rather think not, but you might be able to sell the story to a newspaper.'

'Will that make me rich?' the young lady enquired, getting to her feet.

'Very probably,' Harry replied, 'but I think you should wait until the building is completed, by which time you may no longer need the money.'

Looking somewhat displeased with the answer, she excused herself from our table. The waiter came back with the bill.

'Wow, that was amazing,' I exclaimed.

'What – the girl or the conversation?'

'No, her legs, for heaven's sake.'

Harry pushed the small piece of paper towards me. 'So's this... Exorbitant! That young lady looks like she's getting rich much faster than we ever shall.'

It turned out to be quite a memorable evening, although some of our party may wish to forget their dreadful hangovers. So much for our early night!

Two days later Harry arranged to meet a friend, Hal Pearce, for lunch at the Caspian Hotel. Around noon we jumped into a taxi and went to meet him. The hotel was situated opposite the US Embassy, and Hal was waiting for us in the entrance. Harry introduced me and explained that he and Hal had known one another for many years.

After we had been shown into the dining room and served our delicious lunch, Harry asked Hal to explain to me what he was doing in Iran.

'Well, I've been working here for several years as Chief Quantity Surveyor for the Iranian Gas Trunk Line project known as IGAT. At present, natural gas produced from the oil fields near the Persian Gulf has been flared off as a waste product. IGAT will transfer this gas up to Tehran and various other cities along its path. It can be used there as a domestic and industrial heating fuel. From there it will be transported across the Alborz Mountains to the border of the Soviet Union for consumption in the cities of the Southern Caucasus. In exchange the Russians will pipe their own gas through Czechoslovakia to Western Europe, thus introducing a measure of economic integration between the Iranian, Soviet and Western European economies.'

'I see,' I said. 'So if the Iranians turn the gas off, the Russians turn off the gas they're exporting to Western Europe?'

'That's the general idea, but the Russians want our hard currency, so it would make little sense.'

By the time Harry had explained all about the project for the proposed NIOC headquarters building, our meal was finished. Hal insisted on settling the bill.

'John, would you care to join us for lunch at our house next Friday lunchtime?' Hal asked.

'That's very kind of you. Yes, it'll be a real pleasure.'

'That's fixed, then.' Hal handed me a business card and scribbled his private address on the back. 'And don't forget to bring a bathing costume if you'd like a dip in the pool.'

5

A DAY AT THE RACES

To wisely live your life, you don't need to know much
Just remember two main rules for the beginning:
You better starve, than eat whatever
And better be alone, than with whoever.

Omar Khayyam

Mahin:

The past week had been rather turbulent, and I found that I was becoming a little anxious each time my telephone rang. It was almost as if I knew something momentous was due to happen and suspected it would come through a call, much like the news of Azar had arrived. My mind was repeatedly drawn back to that encounter with the Assyrian woman and all she had predicted for me. And suddenly, as if I had willed it to happen, the phone rang.

'General Jahanbani here. How is Miss Rashvand this morning?'

I allowed myself to breathe, thankful that this was work.

'I'm just fine. What can I do for you, General?'

'I understand that His Majesty has reshuffled his cabinet again and you now have a new minister?'

'That's correct. General Zahedi has been moved to the post of Interior Minister, so it's all change again.'

'And you're still sitting in the same seat? That is truly remarkable. Most incoming ministers bring their secretaries with them. I'm really impressed. How do you do it?'

'I have my little secrets.'

'You're a very astute operator, I know, but let me come straight to the point. I need to meet your new minister. I'm encountering all kinds of difficulties on my estates, and I really need to review matters. Can you fix me an appointment?'

I checked the diary. 'How about the day after tomorrow at about noon?'

'That would be perfect.'

'Before I confirm it, let me just ask the minister if he's willing to receive you. Please hold the line a moment.' I rang through to the minister. 'Yes, he's happy with that. I look forward to seeing you then.'

After this I found I adjusted back into my professionalism, scolding myself for my wandering attention.

Two days later there was a knock at my office door.

'Come in!'

It was General Jahanbani, looking very tall and handsome in his military uniform. 'Good morning. I know I'm a few minutes early.' He pulled an envelope out of his breast pocket. 'These are for you: 12 complimentary tickets to the horse races and polo matches next Friday afternoon. Admission is by invitation only. Bring your sisters along and as many friends as you please.'

'That's very kind, General. What have I done to deserve this honour?'

'You don't need to have done anything. The honour is entirely mine.'

'My sisters and our friends will be absolutely delighted. I can hardly thank you enough. Are you ready to see the minister now? I'll just check and see if he's able to receive you.'

This was a delightful surprise, and I couldn't wait to call my friends to give them the news. The following day I realised that I still had one unallocated ticket and decided to call up my American tutor, who taught me English at the Iran-America Society. 'Betty, Mahin here. How are you – and how's life with your Iranian husband?'

'Just fine thanks, and Bahram is fine, but he's away and won't be back until later next week. What can I do for you?'

'What are you doing next Friday afternoon?'

'Next Friday afternoon… I've nothing special planned. Why?'

I'm going with friends to the horse races, and I'd love you to come. I have complimentary tickets. Can you make it?'

'Why, that would be wonderful!'

'OK, we'll call and pick you up at around two. Will that be all right?'

'Great, I'll be waiting for you.'

John continues:

The following Friday, I knocked on the door of a two-storey townhouse in north Tehran with a bunch of flowers in one hand and a bag containing my swimming trunks and towel in the other. Hal opened the door and ushered me through to the back of the house to the swimming pool, where his wife, Veronica, was waiting.

'Swim first or drink first?'

I noticed several glasses laid out on a nearby table.

'I think I might float higher in the water on an empty stomach.'

'I'll tell you what,' Hal said, pointing towards an open glass door. 'If you pop in there, you can get changed ready for a swim.'

Minutes later I dived in. 'This water is unbelievably warm. Who lives upstairs?'

'Our landlord. This is quite a typical arrangement in Tehran. They build what they call two-storey villas, then let out the ground floor and live upstairs. By so doing homeowners can easily cover the mortgage and other outgoings.'

'Are you going to pour us a drink?' Veronica enquired.

Hal manoeuvred himself out of the pool and disappeared inside the house for a moment.

'Beers all round?'

Veronica produced a large bowl of pistachio nuts.

'There are lots of good things to be had in this country, and pistachios are one of them.' Veronica looked at me. 'How are you enjoying the Iranian cuisine?'

I dragged my body from the warm water and began to dry off.

'Well, I only arrived four days ago, so I'm no expert, but yesterday evening I dined on huge prawns followed by a pepper steak and ice cream in the garden of the Xanadu restaurant. It was absolutely delicious.

'You know, that place is owned by a White Russian émigré,' Hal said, 'a member of the Russian aristocracy. She ran away from Russia during the revolution. There are quite a lot of them living in Iran.'

Veronica obviously enjoyed the subject of food. 'Even though we've lived here for some time, I must admit that cooking Iranian food remains beyond my abilities. The best dishes – similar to what we Brits would call stew – are known as *koresht* in Farsi. They are as delicious as they are complicated to make. Most Iranian dishes are eaten with rice, and once you've tasted rice the way the Iranians cook it, you'll never want to eat it anywhere else. They are the masters.'

'What are we having today, then?' I enquired. The swim had certainly given me an appetite.

'We're going right back to dear old England: roast lamb and mint sauce with roast potatoes and a selection of vegetables,' Veronica declared.

'Couldn't be better! Such a dish is enjoyable anywhere. Have you made a wide circle of friends since you arrived?' I asked.

'Well, most of our friends are linked to the office one way or another, but that does include quite a few Iranian families, mostly among the engineers. The great thing about the Iranians is that they're extremely hospitable, especially towards foreigners. They're very outward looking and interested in other cultures. And they're very keen to practise their English, which is just as well for us.'

The lunch was wonderful, and I settled back comfortably. Just as Veronica was serving coffee, the doorbell rang. Hal went to answer it and came back a few minutes later. 'Our landlord is outside with his family. He has invited us to the races for the afternoon.' Hal looked at his wife and then at me.

'No dissenters, then. I'll take that as a yes.'

Hal introduced me to his landlord, and everyone piled into two cars and drove off to the racecourse on the western outskirts of the city. Much of Tehran in those days resembled a massive building site as it spread its tentacles further and further in all directions. This was especially true of the western suburbs which were fast being transformed into homes for the middle and professional classes. As a rule of thumb, the richer members of society lived higher up the slopes towards the mountains, while the poorer masses lived in the south of the city near the railway station, which was especially oppressive in the summer months.

On arrival at the racecourse, Hal's landlord called us all together. 'Entrance is by invitation only, and I have tickets for everyone.' He led the way through to the front of the stadium, where we sat down on the lower tribunes.

I began studying the programme. Looking over his shoulder, Hal explained, 'You see the horse and its rider on the front of the programme, John? That is His Royal

Highness Prince Hamid Reza, the shah's half-brother and patron of the Iranian Jockey Club. If you look behind, a little higher up, he's sitting with his friends on that section of the tribunes decked out with cushions and Persian carpets.'

I turned my head and then looked back at my programme. 'It seems to be written back to front?' I tried to work it out. 'What a European would consider the back cover is the front cover in Farsi, while what an Iranian would consider the back cover is in English.'

'That's how they write a programme in two languages, so it can be written and read in opposite directions,' Veronica explained. She went on to outline how the afternoon would be organised. It appeared that the horse races would be interspersed by a series of polo matches. During the polo matches, punters could wander around behind the tribunes and place their bets with the bookies.

I had never been to the races before and was curious to inspect the horses before they ran. Maybe I could identify a possible winner. However, I became rather distracted – not by the legs of the horses, but by a line of decidedly glamorous young ladies sitting in a row behind us higher up the tribunes. The racing began, and I found it difficult to concentrate – it was all over in a flash. And as for the polo matches, I confess to not being terribly interested in supporting either side.

Fortunately, Veronica was sitting just behind me, so I had an excuse to turn round when talking to her. After a while, she noticed that my eyes were not entirely focused on her. She looked over her shoulder to see what the fascination was, and when she turned back, she was smiling.

'Good heavens above. So that's what's distracting you!'

'Well, you must admit, they are rather stunning.'

'Ooh, they're looking at us too! And I think they're talking about you.'

'Why? What's wrong with us?'

'Don't be daft. There's nothing wrong with us; it's obviously your blond hair and blue eyes that are the attraction.'

'Really?' I asked. 'What's so remarkable about that?'

'Don't be so dumb, John. Blond hair and blue eyes are as scarce as hens' teeth in this part of the world. Add in that you're a foreigner, you're alone and you're probably earning a good salary, and I'd say the attraction is obvious. What else have they got to talk about?'

Surreptitiously, I peered round again. Three of them were staring straight at me! I looked away quickly and whispered to Veronica.

'But surely they're married… or have boyfriends?'

'What, in this non-permissive society? Married maybe, but boyfriends almost certainly not. Boyfriend–girlfriend relationships are frowned upon, or worse.'

'So how does it work here?'

'Traditionally most Iranian marriages are still arranged between families. But in recent years Western influence has crept in a little. There are certainly more opportunities for girls to choose for themselves. If they come across an attractive candidate, they'll very likely grasp him. If you take my advice, I'd keep your eyes firmly on the horses.'

'Very good advice, I'm sure.'

I turned my eyes back towards the track as the horses hurtled past and then took another look at my programme, but there was nothing in it that could hold my attention. After a while, boredom, stiff legs and the distraction on the upper terraces persuaded me to stand up and take a walk around at the back of the tribunes. As I turned to walk up the gangway, I instinctively glanced to my left. Immediately I caught the eyes of the four young ladies who were staring straight at me. This degree of female attention was seriously disrupting my composure.

Once behind the tribunes I thought about the ladies. One looked European, while the others were clearly Iranian; they could possibly have been sisters. One had lighter hair, possibly dyed, while the one next to her had a look of Claudia Cardinale. But there was one that had especially caught my attention. She had black hair and black eyes and, in my estimation, was very beautiful – almost an Iranian Sophia Loren. Shuddering, I realised how tense I was, almost as though I had caught a chill. I thought back to my heartbreak in France, when I fell in love with my hostess. *Could it be that this girl...?* I dared not complete the sentence in my thoughts for fear of possible disappointment – yes, *disappointment*, I repeated to myself without really thinking what exactly I might mean.

Mahin continues:

'Look, there he is!' Azar squealed in my ear.

My sister Nezhat leant across in front of Parvin, our

other sister, who was sitting on my right. 'That's him! It's got to be! He really does have blond hair, and his eyes are blue.'

'And he's alone. Do you think he's American?' Azar added enthusiastically.

Irritably, I turned on both of them. 'Please be quiet. In any event he's down there, and we're up here.'

Betty, who was sitting at the end of the row, had been following the conversation. 'If you all just hush, I'll listen and see if I can hear an American accent.' We waited in silence, and after a few moments she concluded that he might be Swedish.

At that moment, he stood up and walked up the gangway, and as he passed, our eyes met. He didn't smile and nor did I, but there was no mistaking the intensity of his glance.

'I have a plan.' Betty looked gleeful. 'Before he comes back, let's all move down one level and get a bit closer, and we may be able to start up a conversation.'

I confess that I felt a little apprehensive. It wasn't that I didn't want to meet this young man, but I felt uncomfortable that I had a destiny that appeared to be outside my control. But surely there would be no harm in speaking to him. It really might mean nothing at all. Betty, fired with enthusiasm, led the way, and we all moved closer to where the young man had been sitting. A few minutes later he returned and began talking to the lady in the row behind.

'May I borrow your programme please?' Betty, leaning forward, asked in a broad American accent.

'By all means,' the young man answered, handing Betty his programme while moving one step higher.

'Have you got any good tips?' Betty continued.

'If you find me a space to sit down, we can look at this programme together,' he suggested.

'Why, yes, come right on up.' Azar moved along, thus allowing me to create a space for him between me and Betty.

'I'll let you have it back shortly,' Betty added, opening his programme.

'No rush.'

'Have you placed any bets?'

'Well actually, no,' he replied. 'Have you got any good tips?'

'My friends have.'

'Name's John,' he said, offering his hand to Betty.

'I'm Betty. This is Mahin, and next to her Azar, then Parvin, Nezhat and Frida.'

John stood up and offered his hand to each of us in turn. I thought I had better speak to him myself.

'Are you American?' I asked.

'Well, no, British actually.'

'Where are you staying?' Betty asked.

'Right here in Tehran.'

'What – in a hotel?'

'No, I'm staying in a house in the city centre.'

'What's your job then?' I enquired.

'Ah, that's a little more complicated to explain. I work in the construction industry, and my profession is construction economics. I'm in Tehran to advise on the proposed construction of the new NIOC headquarters building.'

John continues:

At that moment Veronica, who had excused herself just after I returned, reappeared and raised her eyebrows at me. She was no doubt querying how quickly I had discarded her advice.

'And what about you, Betty? You're evidently a long way from home. What are you doing in Iran?'

'I'm married to an Iranian engineer, but I also have a job as an English teacher at the Iran-America Society. In fact, Mahin here is one of my students.'

'How long are you staying in Iran?' Mahin asked.

'About seven weeks,' I explained. 'And what about you, Mahin? What do you do?'

'I'm a minister's secretary.'

'And which minister would that be?'

'The minister of agriculture.'

I raised my eyebrows. 'I guess you must have a very responsible job.'

'Hey!' Betty exclaimed. 'Look, this is the last race. Let's watch! We've got some money on these horses.'

For a few minutes everyone sat in silence, all eyes trained on the track. Betty was on her feet now, revealing a copy of the programme that she'd been sitting on for the last several minutes.

'Come on, number seven! Come on, go for it!' she shouted.

Number seven came in third.

'Oh dear, it's not my day.'

Betty dropped back down onto the cushion she'd placed on the tribune.

'No, it's definitely not my day, and now it's all over. I'd better give you back your programme, John.' She looked over to where Mahin and I were engrossed in our private conversation. 'Ah… Before I give it you back, I'll write Mahin's telephone number on it for you. Mahin, what's your office number?'

Mahin recited her phone number while Betty wrote it down and handed it to me.

I looked at Mahin. 'May I call you in the morning?'

'Sure,' she replied. 'Whenever you like.'

Everyone said their goodbyes, and I rejoined Veronica, who was just getting up from her seat. Veronica just looked at me without saying a word; she was aware it was far too late for any wise advice.

6

IN A PERSIAN GARDEN

Loneliness and solitude are two different things. When you are lonely, it is easy to delude yourself into believing that you are on the right path. Solitude is better for us, as it means being alone without feeling lonely. But eventually it is better to find a person, the person who will be your mirror. Remember, only in another person's heart can you truly see yourself and the presence of God within you.

Mevlana Jalaludin Rumi

John:

Next day I lost no time in calling her.

'Hello, Mahin. John here. Is it convenient to talk?'

'Hello, John. Yes, of course.'

'I thought you might be busy with your minister.'

'No, he has a guest right now, and since I have several phones on my desk, he can interrupt me whenever he wishes, like you've just done. But you're welcome anyway.'

'It was a real pleasure to meet you yesterday. How about dinner later?'

'John, I'm sorry but I can't tonight.'

'How about tomorrow night then?'

'No, I can't tomorrow night either. I'm terribly busy right now.'

'When can you make some time then?'

'I've exams all week long. Thursday will be the first opportunity.'

'I see. I'll call you later in the week to arrange a time and a place then.'

'Yes, that'll be fine. Bye for now.'

I put the phone down, feeling strangely despondent. I would just have to be patient. To that end I endeavoured to become better acquainted with my office colleagues. I had noticed an English lady who was working as a secretary to the Iranian architectural practice. As I walked past her desk, I was surprised to hear her speaking fluently in Farsi.

I was very interested to get to know more about how people lived in this remarkable country, so later that day I introduced myself to her.

'Hello, I'm John.'

'Hello, John.' She smiled at me. 'I'm Caroline. Good to meet you.'

'I heard you speaking Farsi earlier. I was just wondering if you were a student of oriental languages?'

'Not particularly. I am secretary to the senior partners here; I deal with all their correspondence in English.'

'How did you come to learn Farsi so well?'

She looked around, possibly to ensure we were not overheard.

'Well, I came to Iran several years ago having given

up on Englishmen, I suppose. They were either poor or not really worth marrying. Who on earth wants a life struggling to make ends meet? So, I came here, learned the language, found a job and in due course a husband.'

I was amazed. 'You mean you're an unashamed gold digger?'

'Oh yes, guilty as charged. Absolutely.'

'And what's it like being a wife to an Iranian?'

'That's a big question.' She smiled at me and indicated that I should sit down.

'Well… Let me think. I enjoy a good lifestyle, but of course, the cultural differences are considerable. Iranian men have very different expectations than, say, an Englishman would have. Families and family values play a big role in Iranian society. It can be quite burdensome and overly intrusive, if you know what I mean. On the positive side, Iranian hospitality is legendary, and they have a very profound and ancient culture. But the way they think and react is sometimes difficult to decipher.'

She looked at me to see if I understood, but I just shook my head.

'Allegedly they are great lateral thinkers – you'd be amazed. They're a very proud people; they hate losing face or being contradicted.' I could tell she was enjoying her authority on the subject, though there was a touch of bitterness in her tone. 'On the one hand,' she continued, 'they're very friendly, while on the other if something goes wrong, it's never their fault – they'll always find someone else to blame. It can be absolutely infuriating.'

'To the point of dishonesty, you mean?'

'Possibly, but it tends to be subtler than that. I wouldn't call them generally dishonest, but it appears that they prefer to tell people what they believe they want to hear than what we'd consider a straight answer. They prefer not to disappoint. That doesn't mean that what they tell you is necessarily a lie, but it can be very far from what an Englishman would consider appropriate in the circumstances. In fact, I have found myself criticised for saying no when I should find a way to say yes.'

'That sounds somehow familiar. I guess the Protestant ethic encourages us to call a spade a spade, but it's not always tactful.'

'Indeed. It's generally better, rather than saying no, to say, for example, "I think you would be better advised to do such and such …" But you see, an Iranian, in some instances, wouldn't hesitate to tell you what we might call a noble lie rather than the outright truth.'

'How do I learn to tell the difference?'

Caroline laughed softly. 'I guess you'll have to try living with them for a while.'

At that point someone came along to speak with my informative colleague, and I had to take my leave. But I was grateful for her insights, and I determined to learn all I could to expedite my cultural immersion.

The following Tuesday I received excellent news: a telegram from England informed me that I had passed my final examinations and could now apply for my professional diploma. Elated by this success, my first thought was to call Mahin.

'Wonderful news – I've passed my final exams. How

about meeting on Thursday afternoon – say four o'clock in the lobby of the Caspian Hotel, opposite the US Embassy?'

'I'll try and be there by four… I can never be quite sure what time I'll get away from the office, so please don't be surprised if I'm a little late.'

'No problem, that's fine. See you then.' I hung up happily. Now I had two reasons to celebrate!

That afternoon I looked through my limited wardrobe in some dismay. I selected a suit and two pairs of trousers to take to the dry cleaners, ensuring they would be ready for collection by Thursday morning. I was determined to present myself as a well-dressed, respectable Englishman.

Around three o'clock that Thursday afternoon I walked along Shah Reza Avenue and then turned into Pahlavi Avenue. The afternoon was quite warm, and I was grateful for the shade of those protective trees. I swung my jacket over my shoulder in an attempt to blend in with this fashionable area. Many of the younger women shopping were quite stunning. A colleague had once described to me what he called the 'low-slung chassis' of the Iranian women, and the phrase had stuck in my mind. My eyes were drawn downwards, and I found myself wondering whether their hips really were formed a little lower than that of European women.

It was impossible to ignore the contrast in the way people were dressed – women in the latest European fashions intermingled with others covered in full-length veils. Occasionally one of the veils slipped, revealing a beautiful face and elaborate hairdo. The citizens of Tehran, I concluded, constituted two societies: the traditional, religious one and the Westernised, mostly secular one. If the city of Berlin was divided by a wall, then Tehran was divided by two distinct cultures. Little did I realise it then, but just 10 years on, the world was to discover that these two societies living side by side would be as unsustainable as the Berlin Wall also proved to be another 10 years after that.

It was almost four o'clock when I turned right into Avenue Roosevelt and headed towards the US Embassy compound. On entering the Caspian Hotel, I glanced around and confirmed that Mahin had not yet arrived. Choosing a seat that afforded me a good view of the entrance, I ordered an American coffee and a glass of cold water. I confess I felt a little nervous.

Thirty minutes went by, and there was no sign of Mahin – but she had told me that she could be late. Then another 30 minutes passed, and I found myself a copy of the *Tehran Times*, published once a week in English, to distract myself. Would she actually come? This, after all, was the land of arranged marriages; this kind of date was frowned upon. Maybe Caroline was right, and Mahin – not wishing to disappoint me – had told me what I wanted to hear! By half past five I had read the *Tehran Times* from cover to cover, and I ordered a soft drink to pass the time. By six o'clock serious doubts had set in. She probably wasn't going to show up, but as I had nothing else to do, I may as well wait a little longer.

Then I saw her. She was standing in the doorway looking around. The lobby of the hotel, which also served as the hotel lounge, had just begun filling up, and almost immediately there seemed to be a hush around the room, all eyes turning as she walked towards me.

I was quickly on my feet, and I offered Mahin my hand. My pulse quickened at the sight of her. She was even more beautiful than I remembered. And she had made a special effort with her outfit of green blouse, black skirt and a tight-fitting red belt around her tiny waist.

She spoke first. 'I'm so sorry to be late, but the office was very busy, and I simply couldn't leave before my minister.'

'I quite understand,' I replied, offering her the seat opposite. 'There's no need to apologise.'

'Have you been waiting long? I wanted to go home and change, but it was already so late. I came here straight from the office. It's so nice and cool in here.'

She opened her handbag, and while she fumbled around inside looking for something, I sat and watched her, enthralled. Her hair was tied in a ponytail on the top of her head, and it fell, black and silken, to brush the top of her shoulders. Her features were striking: high cheekbones, slightly olive complexion and perfect forehead. But what I found utterly captivating were her remarkable almond-shaped eyes. Although large, they were in perfect proportion to her face. They were accentuated by her large eyelids – a work of art in themselves, immaculately made up with black eyeliner and mascara to emphasise her almost-black irises. Her nose appeared somehow pharaonic. I watched as she produced a pair of earrings from her bag and put them on. Catching my admiring gaze, she smiled at me, and her red lips parted to reveal a row of perfectly white teeth.

I felt like I was in the presence of a Hollywood star. I was sure that I had never set eyes upon such a beautiful creature in all my life.

Inadvertently, I spoke my thoughts aloud. 'You're just so beautiful!'

'Thank you,' Mahin whispered, almost timidly. Momentarily disconcerted by her sincerity, I looked away. We were silent while I regained my composure.

'May I offer you a drink?'

'A Pepsi, please.'

Maybe she doesn't drink alcohol. 'Do you mind if I drink a beer?'

'No, of course not,' she exclaimed, evidently surprised by the question.

I called the waiter over and placed my order.

Mahin continues:

The waiter arrived with the drinks, and while he was searching his pockets for his wallet, I had an opportunity to appraise my date. His colouring was wholly disconcerting. I had had a great deal of time to imagine what my predicted blond-haired boyfriend might look like, but John was unlike anyone I had seen before. His hair looked like spun gold. I would have loved to touch it, but I knew it would be inappropriate. His paler skin tone made him stand out, and when he looked at me, I found it hard to hold the gaze of those clear blue eyes without looking away.

He was more than attractive; he was magnetic and seemed to already have some hold over me. Yet I shouldn't forget that his time in Iran was temporary. Was I being foolish for agreeing to meet him? What if he was the man I was destined to be with – or worse, what if it was all nonsense but I actually fell in love with him and then he left? I admonished myself for racing ahead. This was one date and may mean nothing – I knew that. Yet why was my hand shaking?

I looked up at the very moment he was looking at me. Those blue eyes piercing right through mine. We were silent for several seconds.

'So where in Iran does your family come from?'

I gathered my composure and felt on safer ground.

'My family comes from Ghazvin and many centuries ago from Alamut. Do you know where Ghazvin and Alamut are?'

'I can't say I do.'

'Ghazvin is about two hours' drive west of Tehran. About four hundred years ago it was the capital city of Iran. Alamut is the name of a river valley and a famous 11th-century Ismaili fortress high in the Alborz Mountains accessible by a mountain track from Ghazvin, sometimes known to Europeans as the "Valley of the Assassins". That is where my father's family comes from and where, until some centuries ago, my ancestors lived.'

He looked genuinely interested, which was a very good start.

John continues:

'So you're descended from the legendary Assassins? An *houri* from paradise – the ones described by Marco

Polo in his *Travels*?' She would fit that description perfectly.

'Well, maybe, but I don't really consider myself one, and besides, killing people isn't my line of business.' Mahin smiled, gauging my reaction. 'And what about you, John?' I watched as she sucked the drink through her straw.

'The *houris* didn't kill people, Mahin. Rather they stole the hearts of young men. Maybe that's your business?' I replied.

Mahin looked straight at me with her seductive smile.

'My credentials are far more modest,' I continued. 'My father is a dental surgeon, and my mother a physiotherapist, and our families have lived for centuries in a part of England just west of London. I don't know what else you'd like to know,' I replied. 'What about your father, Mahin? What does he do?'

'He's an industrialist. He manufactures spare parts for internal combustion engines, especially fuel pumps.'

'That sounds complicated. Does he live and work in Tehran?'

'Yes, his office and works are down in the south of the city, but I never go there. I really don't know much about what he does exactly.'

'So, your family is from Ghazvin, but now you're living in Tehran? What did your family do in Ghazvin?'

'My paternal grandfather was an army officer as well as being head of his tribe. My maternal grandfather had hundreds of horses. He used to run the city taxi service – horse-drawn carriages! As for my mother's family, they owned lots of orchards and many local flour mills. But the mills no longer exist. When I was a teenager in Ghazvin, there was no secondary education for girls, so we all moved to Tehran.'

Though I struggled to focus on her conversation, I found myself constantly distracted by her eyes, her hair, the way she moved as she spoke.

When she paused, I was ready with another question: 'And brothers and sisters?'

'There are seven of us, although my mother gave birth to 12 children – but some didn't survive. So, I have three brothers and three sisters.'

'And what do they all do?' I couldn't help feeling that this was going well.

'My eldest brother was educated in France and still lives in Ghazvin. Today he is one of the largest chicken farmers in Iran. He sends about 35 thousand chickens to market every week! My elder brother qualified as an agricultural engineer in Texas, specialising in cotton production. Today he is manager of the largest cotton ginning factory in Iran. My youngest brother, Fereydoon, helps my father in his factory and plays his violin in the National Symphony Orchestra.'

She stopped and looked at me, quizzically.

'And what about you, John? Do you have any brothers or sisters?'

The question caught me off guard and I struggled to regain my focus. 'Only one brother, who has just got married. That's about all I can tell you. We only have small families in Europe.' I paused. 'Your English is very good, Mahin. You must've been studying it for many years.'

'Yes, I have, but I make a lot of mistakes, and my vocabulary is limited. Do you speak French, John? Maybe we could continue in French sometimes? Before the Second World War we used to speak French in Iran as a foreign language. Of course, that was long before I was born, but my father learned French instead of English.'

'Of course. Is that what you're studying at university?'

'My studies are very broad. Apart from modern languages, English, French and Farsi, my favourite subject is biology and human anatomy. My real expertise, however, is in my mother tongue, Farsi. I draft most of the minister's letters for him.'

'That's a lot of typing.'

Mahin's face assumed a haughty expression and I assumed I had inadvertently offended her. 'John, I don't type. I've several typists who work under my direction. When the minister's mail comes in, I write the answers, and quite often he sees the typed-up replies at the same time as the original letter. Then he can sign them off simultaneously.'

'But how do you know what to write?' I enquired, somewhat surprised at this procedure.

'That's the secret of my success at the ministry. I've been there for seven years. I'm now on my third minister, and I'm very familiar with what goes on. A good secretary can read her boss's mind and anticipate what needs to be done before he's even given it a thought.'

'You mean you do the thinking, and he just signs.'

'More or less, yes, that's how it is.'

'It sounds to me like you're in a powerful position. The minister could almost become your puppet.'

Mahin smiled. 'Oh yes, almost everything goes across my desk. I hold the key to the minister, and lots of people attempt to cultivate ministerial favours through me, but it's not easy. It's not just anybody who gets access to the minister.'

'You mean they bring you flowers and things like that?'

'Oh yes, and sometimes much more besides. They can be very persuasive – trying to entice me to accept their gifts, but I nearly always say no.'

I reflected on that for a moment – imagining Mahin behind her desk at the Ministry of Agriculture holding all those admiring men at arm's length. Small wonder she must enjoy her job. I wondered how many of them might be in love with her but dared not reveal their feelings.

'And what about your sisters?' I enquired.

'My sisters? They're all married. You met two of my sisters at the races last week. My blonde-haired sister is married to a general in the Iranian Air Force and my other sister to an officer in the police force.'

'Is she really blonde-haired?'

'To us, yes.'

I watched her eyes as she looked at my own hair.

'Although you may not think so. But she is fairer than most Iranians.'

I paused for a moment. 'Another drink?'

'No thanks.'

But I very much wanted to extend our evening.

'Do you know somewhere nice around here where we can go out to dinner?'

She thought for a moment. 'Yes, we could dine in the

garden of the German Hotel. It's very pretty in spring and summer.'

'Let's go then.'

As we wandered back down Avenue Roosevelt, Mahin slipped her arm through mine. I hadn't been expecting that and wondered whether it was merely a convenience to steady herself on high heels. I slowed my stride down to match hers as she was the only one who knew where we were going. After a pleasant 15-minutes walk, we passed through the iron gates of the German Hotel into a large walled garden. It was dusk, and the lights, which had just been switched on, illuminated the majestic mature trees around the grounds. Tables and chairs were arranged around a bandstand, with a dance floor and a fountain to complete the scene. There were also several swinging hammocks, with thick cushions for couples.

The majority of the guests were Iranian, and as European visitors were still rare at the time, I knew I stood out. A waiter came forward and invited us to take one of these while placing menus on a table in front of us.

'Would you share a bottle of champagne with me?' I suggested, half fearing that Mahin wouldn't drink anything alcoholic. 'I really want to celebrate the results of my final examinations.'

Mahin smiled in acceptance. I asked for the wine list, ordered the champagne and asked Mahin what she would like to eat. When the waiter returned with the bottle and filled our glasses, we both ordered chicken kebab. Picking up our wine flutes, we turned to face one another. I was struggling to hold my glass firmly in my

The authors on their first date dining in the garden of the German Hotel in Tehran

hand, lest Mahin detect the nervous tension running all through my body.

'To your health and happiness, and may all your wishes come true,' I said, touching my glass to my lips. 'That's strange, I'm sure I heard a bird singing... Listen, he's singing his heart out.'

'Birds that sing at night are common in Iran, although I don't know what you call them.' Mahin smiled.

'Ah, you surely mean a nightingale?' I suggested.

'Yes, that must be it. But do you know that it's only the unpaired males that sing at night? He's surely crying his heart out, as you put it, because he's lonely and wants a wife.' I was happy just gazing at her as she spoke. But she startled me with her next question.

'Do you ever feel like that, John?'

She was smiling broadly and looking straight into my eyes. I felt she could read my every thought.

Holding her gaze, I took another sip of champagne, to quell my nerves and plan my answer.

'Well, although it's sometimes pleasant to be alone, being lonely is different. So yes, Mahin, I guess I've experienced such feelings. But with you beside me tonight, I am very much fulfilled. I can only sympathise with the nightingale, poor chap. And wish him happy hunting.' I raised my glass, pleased with my quick-witted response.

The waiter returned with a variety of nuts, crisps, some small salads and chopped cucumbers and yogurt. Mahin began splitting the tiniest nuts with her front teeth.

'What are those?'

'Melon seeds. We've all sorts of nuts and seeds in this country.'

'Mahin, would you believe it if I told you that I'd never even seen a melon until I was about 10 years old? Melons don't grow in England, and after the war we had very little fruit – only apples, pears, plums and some soft seasonal fruit such as strawberries and raspberries. Oranges, lemons, grapes and bananas are all imported. Which melon seeds are those?'

'These are from watermelon. In summer, this country has a surplus of all kinds of melons.'

I put one between my front teeth, trying to imitate what Mahin was doing. But the whole little thing cracked to pieces. Mahin laughed.

'Watch me.' She placed a seed between her front teeth

and swiftly separated the husk from the seed. 'You see it's as easy as that – just like a parrot.'

I wondered if she realised the effect she was having. I made one more attempt with a melon seed before pushing the plate away in exasperation.

'I've had enough of that. It's far too fiddly. I'd die of starvation before I got a meal of melon seeds.'

The waiter arrived with the chicken kebab, and I listened as she spoke to him in Farsi.

'I've asked for some limes. The chicken will have been marinated in lemon juice and various herbs, but we Iranians take lime or lemon juice with just about everything.'

The nightingale began his plaintive song again as I surveyed my surroundings. The night was cool and the air still, scented by the flowers around us. The whole atmosphere of the place was heady and sensual. But most exotic of all was this beautiful woman beside me.

'How do you like the kebab?' Mahin enquired, clearly relishing her own dish. 'One thing about Iranian food is that we use herbs but no hot spices. You should never confuse Persian food with Indian. You won't find any Indian curries in my country, unless of course you go to an Indian restaurant.'

As we enjoyed our meal, I decided to change the direction of our conversation. To explore Mahin's political opinions on the Cold War.

'Iran has several neighbouring countries – Iraq, Turkey, Afghanistan, Pakistan and of course the Soviet Union. Are you not alarmed by the Soviet threat? In the

West we're always concerned that the Russians would like to obtain a warm-water port in the Persian Gulf. Do Iranians trust the Russians?'

When I asked the question, I was hoping to prolong our evening and to learn more of the way that Mahin's mind worked. I wasn't expecting so thorough an answer.

'You know, John, to tell you the truth we don't really care that much for any of our neighbours. At one time or another most of the lands surrounding modern-day Iran were part of the Persian Empire. We have fought with all of them, including the Mongols, who devastated this country in the Middle Ages. With the qualified exception of the Kurds, Armenians and certain Afghan tribes, our neighbours are mostly very different ethnically speaking and have little to compare with our ancient civilisation and culture. We are very wary of all of them. First and foremost, we are Aryans, or if you prefer Caucasian, belonging to the family of Indo-Europeans. Despite our black eyes and olive skin, we consider ourselves closer to Europeans. It's probably no exaggeration to say that ethnically we have more in common with Russians than with any of our immediate neighbours. As for Russian politics and their communist ideals, well, have you read *Animal Farm*?'

'Indeed, I have.'

'Then, you should have realised,' Mahin continued, 'that communism, like all other ideologies promising paradise on earth, is eventually defeated by reality. In our view the Americans are far too concerned about the communist threat. They should pay more attention to those highly dangerous ideologies based on theories promising eternal life in the next world. Warped minds use these as justification for carrying out all kinds of malevolent acts, be it assassinations or even wars. I should know: my own ancestors carried out political assassinations in medieval times in the certain belief of being admitted to paradise. How do you suppose such threats should be addressed?'

'Such as Islam, you mean?'

'Exactly.'

'Mahin, are you suggesting that Islam is a greater threat to Western civilisation than Soviet communism?' The Cold War was at its height at the time, and Mahin had just put forward an assertion which would have bewildered any Englishman.

'Yes, absolutely I am. History teaches us that all civilisations wax and wane. Communism promises the creation of paradise on earth by making all humans equal, but as we all know, that is impossible to deliver in practice. But Islam promises nothing of the sort. It just makes promises about the so-called next life, promises that need never be delivered on earth. Politicians able to convince a population to believe that paradise is attainable in the next world through obedience to their interpretation of correct behaviour in this world would have complete control. Western politicians would be wiser to consider communism as an ideology to be used to restrain the spread of Islam rather than the other way around.'

I was flabbergasted at Mahin's remarks. I took a deep breath in disbelief. Her opinions had just stood the West's strategy towards the Soviets on its head! Little did I appreciate how prescient her assertion would turn out to be in later years, with the collapse of communism and the rise of Islamic terrorism. She seemed to sense the danger even then.

'But, Mahin, no Western politician would ever agree with what you've just said. Any of our politicians who stood up and declared Islam a greater threat to Western civilisation than Soviet communism would be held up to ridicule.'

'Well, just wait and see. Communism as an ideology is unsustainable. It will fail. But Islam will never fail.'

I was stunned. Nervously, I sipped at my champagne.

Mahin continues:

This was a little disconcerting for our first date. Somehow, we had switched from the personal to the political mid-course. But I had very strong beliefs, and if we were to have a future, then I would rather he understood them at the outset.

'Look, John, we know the Russians very well. We've fought them many times. Periodically, they have occupied parts of our country, including my hometown of Ghazvin. In the last century we were forced to cede lands to them. So, on the one hand we don't trust them, but on the other we don't take the communist threat as seriously as you and the Americans do.'

I paused for a moment to take another mouthful of chicken kebab. But I had warmed to my topic, and I hadn't finished yet.

'The conundrum of this country lies elsewhere. Just like you said: Islam.'

'But surely the communist threat is a far more serious matter than your national religion?' John insisted.

'My national religion?' I almost choked on a chicken bone. 'In my opinion, the most disastrous event in our long history was the Arab invasion of Iran in the seventh century. Worse even than the Mongols, who destroyed everything but eventually left, and far worse than anything the Russians have ever done or the Soviets will ever do. Those Arabs destroyed our wonderful Sasanian Empire, the greatest civilisation the world had known at that time.' I took another sip of my drink and looked at this man. He was still gazing at me. I hoped I had not been dominating the conversation too much, but I really needed him to understand. This was too important to me.

'You see, John, in ancient Persia women enjoyed a high level of gender equality, but the Arabs destroyed our equal rights, our freedom of speech and our freedom of religious worship, and in place of our relatively liberal and progressive administration they imposed a brutal system of Islamic government. And this at a time when you Europeans had still not recovered from the aftermath of the fall of the Roman Empire.'

I felt I needed to steady myself. Aware that my resentment was showing, I could feel I was becoming a little emotional.

'Many people disagree with me, but in my opinion my country has been dragged down and held back by this Arab religion. I say "Arab religion" because we Persians don't understand Arabic and consequently can't properly understand the Koran either. This is a religion of foreigners, and it should have no place in my country. After so many years, many of my countrymen remain deeply resentful of the Arab invasion. I know of lecturers of Iranian history who cry bitter tears as they recount this horrific event. But how we'll ever get rid of it, I don't know.'

'Mahin, couldn't we say the same about Christianity? Just like Islam and Judaism, Christianity has its origins in the Middle East. But then Farsi script is the same as Arabic script, surely?' John ventured.

'John, there are many important differences between Christianity and Islam. Christianity has mostly been spread by persuasion and Islam largely by force. As for Farsi script, it looks the same to you, and it is true, it's very similar to Arabic script, but if you ask an Englishman to read the Bible in its Latin or Greek versions, how much will he understand?'

'Apart from the odd scholar of classical languages, precious little,' John replied.

'Well, the Koran is much the same. If you ask 10 scholars to translate it into another language, you'll get 10 different versions, and if you then ask 10 mullahs to explain it, you will get 10 different interpretations. Most people who read the Koran are simply reciting without understanding it, while the clerics are interpreting it to suit their own ends. Do you get what I'm saying?'

John continues:

Mahin had given me a great deal to think about, but at that moment we were interrupted by a photographer who

appeared at the side of our hammock. Mahin reached for my hand and gestured for the photographer to raise his camera. I was a little uncertain as to what was happening, but she moved closer to me and placed one of my arms around her shoulders. I know I must have looked startled, whereas she looked like a film star receiving her press call.

It was all baffling. How had we progressed so swiftly from the formality of our earlier discussions to posing as sweethearts? Immersed in a society renowed for being non-permissive, I was stunned. Yet Mahin had taken the initiative, and it all felt so very natural. The photographer captured the moment and promised to return.

Mahin continues:

As I placed his arm round my shoulders, John seemed to shudder a little. It was bold of me, yet it felt so natural. We had been rather serious in our dinner conversations, so it was a timely interruption. As we posed for our photographs, John's blond hair brushed against my cheek. It was just a fleeting moment, yet I felt strangely intoxicated. Despite my earlier cynicism about my personal destiny, he fitted the profile exactly. And he was so very handsome…

The band was now setting up for the evening: a pianist, two drummers, a violinist and a vocalist, the well-known Elaheh, one of Iran's most popular and talented singers.

I could see John was quite fascinated.

'She looks very glamorous in her colourful dress.'

'John, I've already asked the waiter to request Elaheh to sing the "Kazachok". It's an Iranian version of "Those Were the Days, My Friend", inspired by the original Russian song. Since she knows I asked for it, we should dance.'

'How did you know? That's one of my favourite tunes.' He smiled as he led me towards the dance floor.

John continues:

The orchestra struck up, and we began to dance. Elaheh's voice was divine and its effect almost hypnotic. The tune would have made an evocative soundtrack for a romantic movie. Mahin was confident, spinning around in my arms. I felt a strange, wonderful delirium: a surfeit of emotions. My eyes moistened, and I was unsure whether I was laughing or crying. As the music played on, we alternated between vigorous jiving and intimate waltzes. I didn't remember ever feeling as happy as I did in those moments. I gazed around at other dancers, wondering if they were all experiencing the same ecstasy. Even the trees appeared to play a part, straining at their roots to participate in the spectacle. Mahin had transfixed me. If paradise is anywhere on this earth tonight, I thought, it must surely be right here in this magnificent garden.

After the requested song, we danced on for another 10 minutes or so to the beautiful strains of Shostakovich's famous Second Waltz until, exhausted, we returned to our garden hammock.

Mahin challenged me: 'I saw your eyes watering.'

'Ahh, you noticed?'

'Of course I did. Was it the music or the champagne that made you cry?'

I felt myself redden, and Mahin smiled, holding my hand firmly in hers.

'It's just so romantic here, and the garden is almost as exotic as you are. The music has an extraordinary effect and must surely have been composed in paradise – a happy song sung in a minor key. I've never heard anything quite like it. It brought all my emotions to the surface, and, well, I can't deny it, you saw what happened.'

Mahin squeezed my hand instinctively.

'But you didn't understand the words of her song, did you, John? She was crying about her destiny in life, which had been a complete deception and disappointment.'

'You mean it's not a happy song?'

'No, not really.'

The photographer returned with the photos. Mahin appraised them critically.

'What do you think?' she asked placing them one by one in front of me.

The photographs were stunning. What a startling combination of her dark beauty and my fair complexion. With her arm around me, proprietorially, we already appeared to be a couple.

'I think they're excellent. Two copies of each, please.'

Mahin continues:

In a far corner of the garden, I caught sight of an office colleague sitting alone, and if he hadn't seen me already, it would just be a matter of time before he did. For a moment I considered my predicament: if he were to put the word around the office that he had seen me, the minister's very own secretary, arm in arm with a stranger, there would soon be gossip all around the office corridors. Attack being the best means of defence, I decided I must confront him and dissuade him from mentioning anything he had seen.

I looked at John. 'You must excuse me a moment. I need to speak to someone sitting at another table. Please stay where you are.'

A few minutes later I came back and sat down.

'Who's that?' John asked.

'That gentleman is one of the minister's assistants. I know him very well, but I'm concerned that he doesn't spread stories around the ministry that he saw Miss Rashvand dining out with a young man. I told him that you were a family guest visiting Tehran. He won't believe that, of course, but I now know I can trust him not to talk.'

John continues:

A noble lie, I reflected to myself. 'Is it really that serious?'

'Good heavens, John,' Mahin replied. 'Why do you think I agreed to go out with you tonight? Had an Iranian man asked me, I would never have accepted, unless of course I had a chaperone with me. It's not like Europe here. Marriages are usually arranged, and Iranian men are inclined to think that girls who accept such invitations are, well, let's say "cheap". Any self-respecting girl meeting a young man by way of an introduction would certainly bring at least her sister or brother with her to a date. But with you I've no fears since I know you're not part of this society and you can't gossip in Farsi.'

'You mean that going out with a foreigner is OK, but not with an Iranian?'

'No, neither is OK, but it's OK with me if no one knows. As for the ministry, you wouldn't believe how people's minds work. One day I got in the lift at the top floor of our building to descend to the ground floor. The minister joined me in the lift on the third floor, and the doorman saw just the two of us emerge together unaccompanied at ground floor level. There was gossip all around the ministry for more than a week. What could they possibly imagine we had got up to between the third and ground floor?'

'But that's incredible!' I said, shaking my head in disbelief. 'How can you work like that?'

'With great difficulty. We always have to be careful to see who's in the lift before we get in so that no misunderstandings or scandals arise. Come on, let's dance again!'

The orchestra struck up again and Elaheh's voice rose while Mahin and I danced away as though that magical night would never end. It was nearly midnight when the photographer returned with the photos and I settled his account.

At the gate I asked Mahin if I could see her home.

'Is it a walk, or do we need a taxi?'

'It's a very long walk. Better to take a taxi.'

The doorman called a taxi. We jumped in and 10 minutes later arrived in Aryamehr Avenue.

'I'll see you to your door,' I offered. We walked a short distance up one avenue and turned left into another until we arrived at the garden gate of Mahin's house. Everyone was asleep.

Mahin fumbled around inside her handbag to find the key.

'You can't come in, John, but if you're very quiet, I will let you in just behind the gate. Then you can kiss me goodnight.'

Mahin slowly opened the gate. She crept through and looked around nervously to ensure that no one was awake. Silently, she beckoned me through and closed the gate behind us.

'I live upstairs and my tenant downstairs.' She indicated the house behind her.

'You mean it's all yours, Mahin?'

'Yes, of course.'

Mahin continues:

I took his hands in mine and gazed at him. I wanted to touch his face, kiss the lids of both his perfect blue eyes. But most of all, I wanted to run my fingers through his impossibly fair hair.

'You can kiss me now, and then you must go.'

I felt his hands shaking, and I confess to feeling my own heartbeat quicken at the prospect of our first encounter. John could barely stand still. As he placed his hands around my waist, I took the opportunity I had waited for; I buried my fingers in his soft, golden hair. Then I kissed his eyelids in turn and then moved towards his lips. For a few moments we locked in a passionate embrace.

Reluctantly, I disentangled myself and we stood facing one another.

'It's better you go now. What are you doing tomorrow?'

'It's Friday, so nothing planned.'

'I'll call my brother in the morning, and let's see if we can make a trip up into the mountains. Do you have a phone number for where you're staying?'

'Yes, I do.' He scribbled it down on paper torn from his diary.

'I'll call you in the morning then, but probably after 10 o'clock. Goodnight, John.' I kissed him one more time, with more urgency, then pushed him gently out of my garden and closed the gate behind him.

John continues:

I wandered around the corner and back down the street into Aryamehr Avenue in a daze. I had no real idea of where I was, and at that moment it didn't seem to matter. I pulled a map of Tehran from my pocket and tried to decipher my location. I had about a 30-minute walk back to where I was staying. The temperature was perfect; it was ideal for the walk. It would allow me the time to reflect on the amazing evening I had just spent in that charming garden with the most beautiful creature I had ever met.

7

OVER THE MOUNTAINS

A book of verses underneath the bough
A flask of wine, a loaf of bread and thou
Beside me singing in the wilderness
And wilderness is paradise now.

Omar Khayyam

John:

When the phone did eventually ring, it was already gone 11 o'clock.

'I'm sorry, John, but my lazy brother never gets out of bed before 11.'

Thirty minutes later a car drew up outside, and Mahin emerged from one of the rear doors. Having introduced me to her brother Fereydoon, she gestured that I should get straight in. Sitting in the front passenger seat was Fereydoon's pretty girlfriend, Mahdokht, who turned around to greet me. To my relief, they both seemed very friendly. I confess I had been a little anxious as to her brother's attitude to a Western man going out with his sister. Thankfully my worries appeared groundless, and I was able to relax and enjoy our outing.

'Where are we going?' I asked, placing a kiss on Mahin's cheek.

'First, we're going to Karaj, where we shall need to do a bit of shopping for our picnic, and then we're going to drive up into the mountains and over the top and down the other side towards the Caspian Sea until we find a nice spot to have our leisurely lunch.'

Fereydoon promptly turned his car around and set off along Shah Reza Avenue, heading westwards out of the city, honking his horn at pedestrians and any other vehicle in his way. His car was – like so many others – a locally manufactured Peykan, an Iranian version of the British Hillman Hunter.

'So, you're Mahdokht's chaperone, and Fereydoon is your chaperone – is that right?'

Mahin laughed. 'That's right. But don't worry, we all have the same interests,' she continued, raising her right eyebrow in a suggestive manner.

'And neither Mahdokht's parents nor yours have any idea what's going on, I suppose?'

'Of course not – why should they? We're all adults now.'

Fereydoon began talking to Mahin in Farsi. She interpreted for me.

'Fereydoon says that it's all right for us but not so easy for him and Mahdokht. Her family is Zoroastrian, and her father will only ever allow her to marry a Zoroastrian.'

'And you're Muslim, Mahin?'

'Well, I don't really believe in any religion. I consider myself secular or even an atheist if you like, but my brother and I are considered Muslim – how shall I say – by default.'

'So why doesn't Fereydoon convert to Zoroastrianism, or Mahdokht become a Muslim for that matter?'

Fereydoon, who was managing to follow our conversation, cut in: 'John, what you suggest is unfortunately not possible. It's illegal for a Muslim to convert to another religion. And besides, the Zoroastrian faith does not admit converts. Any daughter of a Zoroastrian who marries outside her faith is considered "lost". She will likely be expelled. I'll explain more about the Zoroastrians when I'm not driving. Like so many religious issues in this country, it's all rather complicated.'

We were clear of the city limits now. The traffic was heavy with cars pouring out of Tehran for the weekend and heavy trucks moving in both directions. The single carriageway road had occasional potholes, causing vehicles to swerve violently towards the oncoming traffic. Mahdokht was screaming at Fereydoon to slow down, to follow the truck in front rather than try and overtake it, while Fereydoon cursed all the black pollution whistling around his windscreen. After about half an hour he pulled over in front of a general store. Once inside, Fereydoon and Mahin began helping themselves to various kinds of fruits, nuts and yogurt as well as some luncheon meat.

'Isn't that pork luncheon meat?' I enquired.

To my surprise, she snapped at me. 'So what? You've got Islam on the brain, John. We call this *kohlbasse*. People can eat what they like, and there is no law against selling it. And do I actually look like a Muslim?'

She looked furious but beautiful. She was wearing a loose-fitting white short-sleeved blouse with a large green and pink flower motif on the front and turquoise-coloured slacks, the two drawn together by a tight-fitting black belt. Her eyes were perfectly made up with eyeliner and black mascara, and through her hair she had tied a blue and white ribbon. Around her neck she had a matching choker in the same material. There she stood, looking magnificently incongruous, in an unpretentious roadside shop half filled with veiled women.

I thought about my own reaction to Mahin, how disconcerted I had been by her beauty. Would I keep her covered up, safe from other men if I could?

'Do I really look like a Muslim?' she repeated. I clearly wasn't getting away without answering. I just shook my head.

'John, would you like some beer or vodka?' Fereydoon asked, taking some bottles off a shelf as if to underscore his sister's point.

'Yes, of course, but please let me pay for it.'

Mahdokht came into the store with several loaves of freshly baked bread she had bought from the baker next door.

'You know what we call this bread, John?' Mahin asked, tearing a piece off the end of one of the loaves Mahdokht was holding. 'We call it *Nan-i-Barbary*.'

'Sounds like barbarian bread to me.'

'That's right – actually it's Russian bread, and when it's hot, it must surely be the most delicious in the world. Here, try a piece.' Before I could answer, she slid a small piece into my mouth.

'Gosh, tastes fantastic.'

'You wait till it's filled with honey and cheese,' Mahin added.

Having loaded everything into the boot, Fereydoon settled with the shopkeeper and took his place behind the wheel. Turning right towards the mountains and driving out of Karaj, we came across several boys selling boxes of fresh strawberries. Mahin signalled Fereydoon to stop and wound her window down. One lad thrust a huge tray containing several kilos of wild strawberries through the car window. Mahin began bargaining. She was very persistent, and Fereydoon soon became impatient. In minutes there were several cars honking their horns behind us. Mahin was unmoved. Even Fereydoon began honking his horn in protest at the delay. But she was having none of it. The boy was protesting loudly for his price, but Mahin soon convinced him to accept a significant reduction.

'They always try to rip off day trippers on Fridays.'

'Especially ones with pretty girlfriends,' Fereydoon added.

Putting the box down in the middle of the back seat, Mahin pressed a strawberry against my lips before inserting it into my mouth. Then she kissed me. Finding my confidence, I began to do the same to her: a strawberry followed by a kiss. It was exquisite. Somehow strawberries interspersed with kisses become even sweeter...

We were beginning to climb now. Fereydoon had to make frequent gear changes as he negotiated steep bends in the road. The higher we climbed the more the road twisted and turned. Then as we came around a very sharp bend, we caught sight of a huge concrete arch dam high above us.

Fereydoon cleared his throat. 'John, behind that dam is the drinking water for Tehran.'

'And washing water as well, I hope.'

We entered a tunnel, and as we emerged, I saw that the road was running along the steep side of a mountain. Far below, a river ran between lines of elegant poplar trees bending with the breeze. We then entered a series of much longer tunnels until we emerged alongside the large reservoir behind the dam.

'We call this the Amir Kabir Dam,' Fereydoon explained, 'and over there to the east are several ski resorts. The highest, with the longest run, begins above an altitude of four thousand metres – that's higher than anything you'll find in the Alps, and it takes a competent skier as much as 20 minutes to ski back down to the bottom of the ski lift. Unfortunately, you've come too late in the year for skiing – the season ends in March.'

We were motoring along beside the lake now, but the mountainsides were so steep as to necessitate several more tunnels, one of which seemed to go on interminably. Finally, we reached a village at the head of the lake. The river feeding the reservoir was a gushing torrent of melting snow. A stream of cars wound their way upwards into the mountains, heading for the pass at the top. Many had stopped for lunch to patronise the numerous cafes and restaurants in the village.

'I can smell chello kebab,' Fereydoon said.

'We can stop for that on our way back this evening,' Mahin suggested as I stuck my head out of the car window to inhale the delicious odours of barbecued lamb and fresh tomatoes.

Gradually the valley broadened out as our car continued its seemingly endless ascent. Eventually we reached another village, and suddenly it was as though we had arrived in a Dutch garden in the mountains: a sea of flowers.

'These flowers we call tulips. It's a Persian word – didn't you know?' Fereydoon volunteered.

High above us the snow-capped mountains were quite spectacular, though my eyes were not focused on the tulips but, as always, on Mahin.

'Look, what gluttony! The strawberries are almost gone.' Unable to respond, Mahin opened her mouth to reveal her perfect white teeth all covered in strawberry juice.

With a mischievous smile on her face, she addressed me teasingly, 'John, dear, would you like a kiss? I think we had better give the rest of the strawberries to Mahdokht so that she can feed the driver.'

Fereydoon pulled over to refuel, stuffing a handful of strawberries into his mouth as he stepped out of the car. A few minutes later we continued winding our way on up the mountain and around a series of hairpin bends. We were surrounded by dramatic steep-sided arid mountain slopes, and in places steel-framed galleries had been erected to protect the road from rockfalls. Eventually we came to a halt in front of a red light at a tunnel portal. Hitherto the sky had been an unblemished blue, but now clouds had appeared along the skyline above the mountaintops.

'One-way system here,' Fereydoon explained. 'We'll have to wait for a green light.'

It took several minutes to drive through the tunnel, and when we emerged at the other end, I was amazed to find it was misty and raining. The mountains this side were even more precipitous, and the hairpin bends even sharper and steeper: one false move and a vehicle would crash into the abyss below. I found myself clutching the sides of my seat, as I looked away from the daunting drop and across at Mahin. She was entirely unconcerned as she chatted to Mahdokht. I relaxed.

Swiftly, we descended below the treeline again and entered another world of lush, damp, wooded hills, passing through deep ravines where the rocky sides of the mountains dramatically overhung the road. Gradually this road widened out and Fereydoon started looking for somewhere suitably secluded for a picnic lunch. Many of the obviously desirable places had already been taken by those who had left home earlier, but his patience eventually paid off. We settled on a grassy bank among the woods; a delightful spot made more relaxing by the sounds of rushing water pouring down from the mountains above.

John and Mahin on their second date: enjoying a picnic next to a raging torrent of water from the melting snow of the High Alborz Mountains between Tehran and the Caspian Sea. (Fereydoon and Mahdokht in a passionate embrace in the foreground.)

The rain stopped, and the sun reappeared, while the temperature in the shade of the clusters of trees was most agreeable. Fereydoon laid out a series of Persian rugs on the grass while I helped the girls lay out the picnic. I took the tops off a couple of bottles of local beer and poured Pepsis for the girls. Mahdokht peeled and cut up cucumbers and radishes and added them to a bowl of yogurt. She then tore the bread apart and invited everyone to eat. Mahin sliced tomatoes and gherkins to put in the bread with cheese and *kohlbasse*.

As soon as he had finished eating, Fereydoon returned to his car and came back with his violin and began playing the first movement of Mozart's *Eine Kleine Nachtmusik*. As

I watched him skilfully playing, it crossed my mind that in a woman's eyes he may have looked as handsome as his sister was beautiful. Lying there, I felt as though I had been transported into another world, but to my horror no sooner had Fereydoon finished playing than Mahin snapped me out of my trance by complaining about the violin. Apparently, she had suffered her brother's endless practice for as long as she could remember.

'I have to practise!' Fereydoon insisted. 'We shall be playing that at the Roudaki Concert Hall in Tehran the week after next. You're all invited to attend with my compliments.' He continued playing some classical Iranian music.

'More nerve-racking scraping of his beastly violin,' Mahin groaned.

'I for one,' I said, 'will be very pleased to accept Fereydoon's kind invitation.'

A while later Fereydoon lay down on one of the rugs, and Mahdokht snuggled up beside him. With her brother wrapped in a passionate embrace with Mahdokht, Mahin lay down on the other rug and intimated to me that we should do likewise. I was as tense as a beanpole as I lay down and kissed her. Placing one hand behind my head to draw me closer, she began exploring my body with her other hand.

'What are you doing?' I asked nervously, wondering what she might do next.

'Checking the goods – I hate being cheated.'

I instinctively recoiled. 'I'm not a slave for sale, Mahin.'

'You might soon be wishing you were,' she replied provocatively.

'Can I check your goods then?'

'Absolutely not! You can kiss me again, but that's all.'

Mahin ran her fingers through my hair as I kissed her. Then, holding my head in her hands, she fixed me in her gaze. I was in thrall to this fabulous girl.

'So, blond hair and blue eyes, eh?'

Mahin pursed her lips, her eyes firmly fixed on my hair. 'Yes,' she said very slowly, before kissing each of my eyes in turn.

'Now your eyes are red all around with my lipstick.'

I looked at her in silent amazement. Her eyes were amazing. The irises were almost as black as the pupils. I could not get over how her eyelids seemed to disappear into recesses beneath her forehead. The high cheekbones and her nose could have belonged to the wife of Tutankhamun. Europeans could easily mistake her for being Spanish, Greek or Italian, but somehow, she looked – how shall I say? – simply more exciting than any European woman I had ever seen. Gazing into her eyes, I felt she was taking possession of my very soul. Then she smiled and raised her right eyebrow as though she understood very well what she was doing.

This woman was supremely self-confident; I could sense the satisfaction she was drawing from a growing sense of power and influence over another human being. She could ultimately use me for any of her own purposes. I felt drawn by two seemingly irreconcilable yet intense opposing forces: security and fear. The sense of security humans crave from being in love, and the fear of its terrifying consequences.

'Mahin, I'm in paradise – stop the clock, right now.'

'If only I could.' She sighed, and grasping my right hand, she rolled over onto her back. 'Now let's sleep a little.'

Mahin continues:

There was perfect silence in this demi-paradise. I listened to the rushing of the melting snow as it hurtled down the mountainside on its way to the Caspian Sea. The torrents drowned out the sound of leaves rustling in the trees above our heads. The burning sun penetrated the foliage and flickered on the ground around us. I tried to sleep, but I was too distracted by John's proximity. As I listened to his measured breathing, I took the chance to think about everything we had done since we had first met. How wonderful it had been dancing close to him; how exquisite our first kiss. But I wanted more of him. I wondered what would have happened had we been alone, and that thought ran as a heat through my veins. My own thoughts were shocking to me; I was far too aroused.

After a little while John began breathing deeply, suggesting that he was perhaps asleep. I turned on my side to look at him. I couldn't believe that this Englishman had come seemingly from nowhere to fall in love with me and I with him. Would this man be my future husband? If he asked me, how should I answer? Or would he fly away again as quickly as he had arrived?

I think I already knew, but I would not tempt fate by answering my own question. Instead, I would kiss him awake.

John continues:

I opened my eyes to see Mahin's beautiful face smiling at me. I immediately raised my hands and put them behind her head, pulling her lips down on mine, and held them there, until very slowly I released her so that she could sit up beside me.

'Tell me more about your life, John.'

'What would you like to know?'

'How did you learn to speak such good French?' she asked.

'Oh, that's a long story, but since you have asked... When I was 13 years old, I was sent to a famous boarding school far from where we were living. At the end of my first term my father was horrified to discover that I had become bottom of the bottom class in French. So, he decided to send me away to France on exchange with a French boy, and the following summertime I spent three weeks staying with a huge family in a large chateau just south of Paris. There were as many as 30 people – uncles, cousins, aunts, brothers and sisters – sitting around the dining table for three meals each day, with three servants and a cook in the kitchen. We dined like lords of the manor. The experience made a lasting impression, and France and everything French transformed me into something of a Francophile.'

'So, you immediately became something of a linguist then?' Mahin interjected.

'Yes, it turned out to be a brilliant initiative on my father's part, so much so that the following summer I decided to do it again but with another family, living in the Pays Basque in south-west France.'

'Sounds absolutely wonderful! Lucky you!' Mahin added, bending over to plant a kiss on my forehead.

I reflected for a moment before continuing. Should I recount my intimate story about 'Madame'?

'Now I'm going to tell you a very personal story…'

And there, on that beautiful mountain, I told Mahin about Francis's mother and how a young boy had become so captivated, and so heartbroken, that her image had remained as the template of beauty to him. I told her, too, about the red ribbon in her hair that seemed to signal the care she had executed in dressing for me.

'You fell in love with her, John. Are you still in love with her?' Mahin asked.

'Mahin, no!' I reached out to touch her face. 'Your eyes and hair are even blacker than hers, and besides, you are much more beautiful.'

Mahin looked relieved and, seeing that my eyes were watering, wiped them with the tips of her fingers.

'To answer your question,' I continued, 'I suppose I shall never forget her for as long as I live. I have developed a tendency to judge all the other women I have met since those days by comparing them with her and have always been disappointed. Until now, of course…'

I smiled. Mahin bent over and kissed me again.

About an hour later, Fereydoon began to stir.

'I promised to tell you about the Zoroastrians,' he began. 'Zoroastrianism is often regarded as the world's original monotheistic religion. It was founded by the prophet

Zoroaster or Zarathustra – in Farsi we call him *Zartosht* – in ancient Iran some three thousand years ago. For more than a thousand years it was one of the most powerful religions in the world, and during the Achaemenid period it became our official state religion. Zoroastrians believe there is one God, *Ahura Mazda*, who created the world and revealed the truth through his prophet *Zartosht*. Some Westerners believe that Zoroastrians are fire worshippers, but this isn't true. Zoroastrians believe that the elements are pure and that fire represents God's light or wisdom. The Zoroastrian book of holy scriptures is called the *Avesta*. Zoroastrian beliefs can be summed up as "Good thoughts, good words and good deeds".

'That sounds like subtle shorthand for the Ten Commandments,' I ventured.

Fereydoon paused for a moment and then offered to try to explain the difference between cosmic and moral dualism.

'Moral dualism in Zoroastrianism acknowledges the existence of a complete separation of good and evil. Cosmic dualism, on the other hand, refers to the ongoing battle between the good, that's *Ahura Mazda*, and evil, known as *Angra Mainyu*, within the universe. With cosmic dualism we have life and death, day and night, good and evil. Life is a mixture of opposing forces, and we cannot understand one without the other.' He paused as he tried to find words in English.

'Moral dualism, on the other hand, refers to the opposition of good and evil in the mind of mankind. The path of evil leads to misery and ultimately hell, while the path of righteousness leads to peace and everlasting happiness in paradise. Moreover, as with cosmic dualism, we have the polarity of happiness and sadness, truth and deception and so on, but with an emphasis on choice.'

'That sounds to me like a very reasonable basis for any kind of religion.'

'Very good point, John,' Fereydoon continued. 'In fact, you're quite right. It's widely accepted that the Jewish, Christian and Islamic faiths were significantly influenced by the concepts of Zoroastrian eschatology: that is to say, life after death, heaven and hell and messianic redemption as well as right and wrong and so on, enshrined in the Zoroastrian religion.'

I reflected for a moment. It would have been so much simpler had human beings universally adopted Zoroastrianism. Just imagine how many religious wars mankind would have been spared, I thought.

Fereydoon continued, 'Zoroastrians also believe that everything God created is pure and should be treated with love and respect. This includes the natural environment, so Zoroastrians traditionally do not pollute rivers, land or the atmosphere. Interestingly, for the same reasons, rather than contaminate the soil or the air, they neither bury nor cremate their dead but cast the bodies of the deceased into what are called "Towers of Silence", where the corpses can be devoured by birds of prey. There are many of these huge austere structures still in existence in Iran today. For these reasons some people even now consider Zoroastrianism as the first ecological religion.'

'What about Nowruz, New Year?' Mahdokht interjected.

'Good point,' Fereydoon continued. 'The Iranian calendar begins every year on the first day of spring, the vernal equinox, usually 20th March. Despite Islam, the Zoroastrian feast of Nowruz remains the most important holiday of the year in Iran today, rather like Christmas in the West. Before the introduction of the Gregorian calendar, most of the known world used the Roman Julian calendar, which itself is widely accepted to have been based on the Zoroastrian one.'

Mahin was sitting now. A mischievous smile played around her lips and she held my hand firmly in hers.

'So, what about Christmas, then? Isn't that Zoroastrian as well?' she prompted.

Mahin appeared to be encouraging her brother to reveal yet more surprising facts. Her excitement was tangible; it was clearly important to her to continue my education on these matters.

'Well, actually, yes, it is. What John will surely find fascinating is the history of the feast of Christmas in the Zoroastrian context. The celebration of Christmas derives from the Persian celebration of Yalda, which occurs on the longest night of the year on the eve of the winter solstice. On the eve of Yalda, Persians used to stay awake all night until dawn, and normally the following days were holidays, 22nd December through the 25th. It was also the "Day of Equality" because on this day it was customary for the monarch and his nobles to dress like ordinary people so as not to be recognised in the crowds. On 25th December, Persians used to celebrate Mithrakana. The birth of Mithra was an occasion when traditionally wreaths of green cypress were hung on doors, gifts presented to loved ones and feasting continued all night long. Many Christian, Jewish and Muslim customs have their roots in Mithraism and Zoroastrianism. The birthday of Mithra was celebrated in ancient Persia, Rome and other parts of Europe as Mithraism spread rapidly throughout the ancient world.'

'So who was Mithra?' I enquired.

'In the Zoroastrian faith, Mithra was a judicial figure, an all-seeing Protector of the Truth and the Guardian of Cattle, the Harvest and the Waters. Most importantly, he exercised the authority that you Christians attribute to St Peter. He decided who went to paradise and who went to hell.'

'Fascinating.' I was very impressed with the extent of his knowledge and his eloquence in its telling.

'Another old tradition was that everyone pledged to plant a cedar tree during the festival of Yalda. That is why Christians put Christmas trees in their houses every year, and it never ceases to amaze me that most Westerners have no idea why they do it.'

He was quite correct in that assumption, it was a tradition that I had never questioned up until this point. Before I could reply, he continued with my lesson.

'The oldest record of the Yalda night celebrated throughout the Indo-European world dates to around 1600 BC. "Merry Mithrakana" gradually became "Merry Christmas" with the spread of Christianity in the Roman Empire. The Catholic priests, being unable to put an end to the practice of celebrating Mithra's birthday on 25th

December, and not actually knowing on which day Jesus was born, effectively hijacked Mithrakana and declared this day to be the birthday of Jesus.'

By this point Mahdokht was busy packing up the picnic and putting items back in the car. Fereydoon, satisfied that I now fully understood the topic, went to turn the car around to head back home. The sun had already disappeared behind the mountains. About an hour later it was almost dark, and seeing smoke rising in the near distance, Fereydoon pulled over in front of a restaurant serving chelo kebab. It was busy inside with day trippers on their way back to Tehran, but eventually we were able to find a small table with four chairs. The girls sat together on one side, and we sat opposite our respective girlfriends.

'Now, John, you can taste the Persian national dish,' Mahdokht explained in her broken English.

'Well, I can certainly smell it,' I replied. Looking around I noticed quite a lot of people drinking a white liquid.

'Why are so many people drinking milk with their meal?'

Mahdokht sniggered and covered her mouth in embarrassment. Fereydoon's face broke into a broad smile.

'It's not milk, John. It's *doogh*, and before you ask me what *doogh* is, I'll explain. It's a mixture of yogurt and carbonated water, often served with ice. Occasionally herbs such as mint are added. It's quite refreshing. Would you like to try some?'

'I think I would prefer it to drinking all that sweet Pepsi and Coke.'

'Chelo kebabs all round, then, with *doogh*?' Fereydoon suggested. We all nodded our approval. The waiter returned almost immediately with the *doogh*, four raw egg yolks in their half shells, some sliced raw onions and butter, a small basket of bread and some form of what looked like brown seasoning.

Mahin offered me a piece of bread. 'Before you start asking questions, we call this flatbread *sang-gak* because it's cooked on stones in an oven. "*Sang*" means "stone" in Farsi. We will explain everything else as it arrives.'

Ten minutes later the waiter returned with four large plates of steaming hot rice garnished with chargrilled onions and tomatoes. He then went back and fetched a large plateful of chargrilled lamb kebab on long skewers.

Mahin picked up one of the egg yolks and tipped it on top of her rice, followed by a pat of butter, and mixed it all up. Somewhat apprehensively I did likewise.

'You see, the butter melts and the egg yolk cooks in the hot rice,' Fereydoon explained. 'There are two kinds of meat, kebab and kubideh. Kubideh is minced lamb marinated in raw onion and lemon juice and various herbs.' He began pushing the meat off the skewers onto his plate. 'We can take one skewer of each kind. Finally, we sprinkle sumac all over everything.'

'Which is?'

'Sumac is a herb produced from the ground fruit of a flowering shrub that we put on some rice dishes to enhance their flavour,' Mahin explained.

'It's absolutely delicious. Somehow, Iranian rice tastes better than any I have ever tasted anywhere in Europe.'

Fereydoon looked across the table. 'Easily explained. Most Europeans have no idea how to cook rice.'

'Indeed,' I added. 'They turn it into either an overcooked soggy pudding or uncooked grit.'

I knocked back the remainder of my *doogh* just as we all stood up before walking to the car. About an hour later we were back in Tehran, where I was dropped off at my residence before Fereydoon drove the girls away into the night. I looked forward to my bed and the chance to relive every moment of this incredible day.

8

THE RUSSIAN CIRCUS

How sad, a heart that
does not know how to love, that
does not know what it is to be drunk with love.
If you are not in love, how can you enjoy
the blinding light of the sun,
the soft light of the moon?

Omar Khayyam

Mahin:

The following morning, I had barely sat down at my desk when the phone rang.

'Mahin, it's Azar here. Now, tell me all about it. Are blond-haired, blue-eyed Englishmen that different? You must have found out by now.'

'You don't really think I'm going to answer that question?'

'You must tell me. I want to know.'

'Why, are you hoping to find one for yourself?'

'I wish I could.'

'You're a married woman. You can't wish for such things.'

'You've been out with him, haven't you? And without a chaperone? Now tell me the truth.'

'To tell you the honest truth, we went out yesterday with my brother and his girlfriend to Karaj, and over the mountains, for a picnic.'

'I'll bet that was delicious.'

'Yes, Azar, the picnic was delicious. Are you surprised?'

'No, not at all, but what happened after the picnic?'

'We had a chelo kebab on the way home, and that was it.'

'When are you seeing him again?'

'Nothing fixed yet. Now I must get on with my work.'

'I'll call you later in the week. Then perhaps your news will be a bit juicier. Bye for now.'

Later that morning John called to thank me and my brother for a wonderful time the previous day. His voice fizzed with enthusiasm. 'I'd never imagined anything quite like it – the mountains and the scale of the vistas were just so impressive.'

I smiled into the phone. His appreciation was so refreshing.

'…and the contrast in the climate from one side of the mountains to the other in such a short distance was truly amazing. It was such a surprise! I had assumed that the Middle East was mostly desert.'

'You should come again in winter next time,' I replied. I paused for a moment, aware that in saying this I'd brought up the topic of his departure. I hurried on, 'While in summer the Caspian coast is almost tropical, in winter it often freezes over, and the entire area is blanketed in thick snow.'

We talked further for a few minutes before he reached the purpose of his call.

'There's a Russian circus in town at the Park-e-Farah. How about going there next Tuesday?'

'Good idea. I'm busy now, though. Call me later in the week please.' As I replaced the receiver, I congratulated myself on not sounding too eager!

John continues:

Later that day I met Caroline in the office corridor.

'Hello, John, have you been told any noble lies yet?'

'Not to my knowledge.'

'Or examples of lateral thinking, perhaps?' Caroline went on.

'Not yet, but I do think that by our standards Iranians do sometimes behave in an unconventional way. I've noticed that they seem to have no hang-ups in discussing intimate matters in an almost childlike manner. That seems in stark contrast to our British Victorian values.'

Caroline's eyes gleamed with curiosity. 'Intimate matters? Who have you been talking to, John?'

'I've made some new friends, and I overheard a conversation,' I lied.

'What – you've learned Farsi already?'

'Someone translated it for me,' I lied again.

'That sounds more like an English noble lie told with a twinkle in your eye.'

I attempted to look innocent.

'Nevertheless, you're right – they certainly have few hang-ups in discussing intimate matters, provided it's not their own intimate matters, but on the other hand, when it comes to formal behaviour, they can be more Victorian than the Victorians.'

I looked at Caroline somewhat quizzically, wondering what she was implying. She continued with her questions.

'What about lateral thinking – about perceiving situations in an entirely different way?'

'No, not yet… I'm not really sure.'

'Let me give you an example. The present British ambassador, Sir Denis Wright, is a quite remarkable man. He understands the Iranians very well and speaks and writes fluent Farsi. In a recent speech he made two rather amusing comments about Iranians.'

'Which were?'

'"If you ask an Iranian which his left ear is, he will raise his right arm over the top of his head and touch his left ear." Bizarre, don't you agree? Secondly, he recounted a story that happened between the wars when Reza Shah, the present shah's father, was expected to visit one of the construction sites along the Trans-Iranian Railway. A few days before he was due to arrive at a certain point along the new line, a small locomotive was derailed and fell on its side. The construction workers pushed and shoved with blocks and tackles and so on, but they simply couldn't move it. Apprehensive at what the shah might say if he saw it, what do you think they did?'

Caroline looked at me, clearly expecting an answer.

'No idea.'

'Buried it in sand: "Another spoil tip, Your Majesty." Can you imagine what Englishman would ever have thought of doing such a thing?'

'That's unbelievable.'

'Isn't it? Anyway, I must go now. See you later.' Caroline disappeared along another corridor.

The following Tuesday morning I called Mahin and arranged to meet her at half past six at the entrance to the Park-e-Farah. At about a quarter to seven she stepped out of a taxi, and I was reminded afresh of how stunning she was. She was dressed in a short-sleeved white silk blouse, a black knee-length skirt, a red leather belt and, most striking of all, a red ribbon drawn through her black hair. Yes, a red ribbon drawn through her black hair!

'You look amazing!' I exclaimed, unable to prevent myself staring at the ribbon. I felt my pulse quicken. I was immediately transported back to France with all the desire that had been awakened in my younger self.

'I've come here straight from the office. I thought I'd never get away.'

'You mean you've been dressed like that all day in the office?'

'Why do you ask? Is there something wrong with it?'

'No, not at all, it's just that you look so glamorous I can't imagine how the minister and his male colleagues can ever concentrate on their work.'

'That's their problem.'

We joined the queue for tickets, and I had the uncomfortable feeling that we were the centre of attention.

The young men around us openly stared at Mahin whilst we received frowns of disapproval from women in chadors. Tickets in hand, we climbed the stairs constructed from wooden planks and scaffold poles to the upper circle of the big top. From here there was a commanding view of the arena. We had hardly taken our places when Mahin's attention was drawn to two small blond-haired children in the row in front of us.

'John, look, aren't they simply adorable! I want two boys just like that with blond hair and blue eyes, and I'll call them Cyrus and Darius after our great Achaemenid kings.'

I was thunderstruck at this remark and replied rather tactlessly, 'But, Mahin, you have black hair and black eyes…'

She looked straight at me. 'But you, John, have blond hair and blue eyes.' At this I was completely lost for words; I was aghast and held on to the arms of my seat to steady myself. Mahin, not the least put out by my reaction, began engaging the boys in conversation. Eventually, their parents joined in.

'What are their names? They're absolutely gorgeous.'

'This is Jan, and this is Dirk,' their mother proudly announced in a thick Dutch accent.

'How old are they?'

'Jan is five and Dirk is three.'

'Their hair is so blond and their eyes so blue.'

'Yes, like their father.'

Mahin craned her head further forward to take a closer look. Unabashed, she deliberately and studiously peered at the boys' blond-haired father, who turned his head to oblige her.

'It's nice being flattered by two ladies at once,' he said half-jokingly.

Mahin was squeezing my hand in delight. She was utterly ecstatic.

'I think you're Dutch.'

'We are indeed,' the husband acknowledged. 'I have a job here in Tehran with Royal Dutch Shell.'

'Do you like living in Tehran?' Mahin went on.

'Yes, we're really happy here. In fact, we'd like to spend many years here, but in my industry, they give us about three years in each posting and then move us on.'

At that moment there was a rumbling of drums as several clowns came cartwheeling into the ring. These were followed by a posse of horses, which trotted round, performing tricks, as their trainer cracked his whip.

But I could see that Mahin's eyes were elsewhere. It was a little disconcerting. She kept leaning forward as if to study the children in detail. Fortunately, the boys were concentrating on the activities in the ring and weren't fully aware of Mahin watching them from every possible angle. It appeared as if she was comparing them first with their father and then with me. Only occasionally did she look over their shoulders to watch the performance. I tried to ignore this rather embarrassing behaviour. She was clearly possessed by maternal instincts. It was only when the high wire act started and I held her hand tightly that she finally began paying attention to the circus act.

When the interval came, Mahin continued doting on the boys. Fortunately, their mother appeared to enjoy every moment of Mahin's attention towards her offspring.

Mahin looked at me, her face illuminated with delight. 'I wish I could take them home.'

'What? You're joking!'

The performance ended around half past nine, and Mahin followed the boys all the way out of the circus enclosure to bid them goodnight. For a moment I worried that she was going to grasp them and kiss them. As we walked away from the circus tent, she repeated her wish again. 'One day soon I really must have two golden-haired boys like that.'

'And if you had a daughter, what would you call her?'

'Mandana.'

'Mandana? Why that?'

'Mandana is an old Persian name meaning "eternal". She was the mother of our greatest king, Cyrus the Great.'

I looked intently at Mahin. 'You seem to have all the answers. How about looking for somewhere to eat?'

We walked for a while along Aryamehr Avenue until we came across a restaurant serving our favourite chargrilled chicken kebab. A waiter showed us to a small table, where we sat down in a secluded corner facing one another.

'You're a very single-minded woman, Mahin. You seem to have an extraordinary sense of self-confidence – self-belief even – as well as the courage of your own convictions. Those are qualities of leadership, and you behave like someone twice your age.'

'But you don't know how old I am,' Mahin retorted.

'No, I don't. Are you going to tell me?'

'No, absolutely not. Why should I? I consider life like

a game of poker: only stupid people put their cards face up on the table, unless of course they have a winning hand. Mystery can be a powerful tool. Keep on guessing.' She laughed. 'My father once said I should become the prime minister of this country. I know what he meant, but it's never going to happen. Had I been born a man, then maybe he would be right. On the other hand, what qualities do you imagine I should have to hold down my present job? I've already survived two changes of minister. I've never wished to leave the Ministry of Agriculture since to do so would carry risks. You wouldn't believe what snake pits these ministries are. Everyone competes for position, power and influence.'

I was constantly impressed by her abilities – and her awareness of her own strengths.

'And do you drive?'

'Oh yes, I used to have a car, a Skoda, until quite recently, when I bought the house. I sold it to buy some furniture. Anyway, since I have a driver who comes and picks me up for work in the mornings, I don't really need one.'

'A driver to take you to work each morning?' I was incredulous. 'You mean the ministry pays for a driver to bring their secretaries to work each day?'

'Not any secretary, John, just me. I don't think you understand what my position in the ministry really is. I'm the power behind – how shall I say – the ministerial throne.'

'Are your sisters like you?'

Mahin began to giggle, her perfect white teeth glistening between her red lips.

'No, John, no one in my family is like me. None of them could ever do my job. I'm a very political animal. I can read people's minds like you read a book. I think fast, and I act fast. I'm always at least one step ahead. That's how I survive and thrive.'

I believed her. I suspected that she had already read my mind. There was something truly extraordinary about this woman. She seemed to possess a rare and intoxicating mix of exceptional beauty and remarkable self-confidence. It was a powerful and disarming combination. She might almost have been a poker player. We were completely different characters: chalk and cheese. I was used to putting my cards on the table, and that had always been my way. I was beginning to realise that Mahin could run circles around me.

'So how come your sisters are married and you're not?'

'Did I tell you I wasn't married?' Mahin retorted. 'You never asked, so why should I tell you?'

Stunned by Mahin's response, I was unsure how to react to this unexpected statement. I had assumed... Perhaps I should not have assumed. But surely she was just joking?

'Well, in case I don't get a straight answer, I won't ask.'

'That's very diplomatic of you. So now at last you're beginning to think like an Iranian,' she teased. 'You're learning. It's always much better to ask questions than to answer them.'

'What kind of a conversation would that make – everyone asking questions and no one providing any answers? It would be like the Mad Hatter's tea party in *Alice in Wonderland*.'

'Of course – full of noble lies instead of truthful answers.'

The waiter arrived with the chicken kebab. Mahin squeezed lime juice and sprinkled sumac all over it and began separating the tomatoes from their skins.

'What would you like to drink, Mahin – Pepsi or *doogh*?'

Mahin looked at the waiter, who was still standing nearby, and ordered two *dooghs*.

'Well then, let me rephrase my question: irrespective of whether you're married or not, how come your sisters are married?'

'That's a pretty dumb question, John. I guess they all got offers and accepted. What else?' Mahin paused. 'I don't think you understand Iranian society. Did I not explain this before? In general terms the girlfriend–boyfriend business that you Westerners practise isn't acceptable here.'

'So, what are we doing here then? If this isn't a girlfriend–boyfriend relationship, what is it? Anyhow, present circumstances aside – how do boys and girls meet?'

'Well, there are various ways. Traditionally a lot of matchmaking goes on, introductions between friends and families. Another way is that young men, escorted by their parents, go from house to house knocking on doors seeking a wife. Some years ago, before my family moved to Tehran, the doorbell was forever ringing. Out of politeness and good neighbourliness my parents were obliged to listen to all that stuff. I always made it clear to my mother and father that I would never marry any man who made that kind of approach. I refused to meet them, and my parents always had to make excuses, saying that I would never agree or that I was sick. Furthermore, we used to make it known that my father drank vodka – which is true – but at least that discouraged the more religiously inclined candidates. I should also add that before they come knocking, some – how shall I say – "spies" will have already found out that there is a pretty girl living in this or that house. Then negotiations begin. Frankly, it's a ghastly business. More lately in Tehran it has become fashionable to find a partner in a cinema queue.'

'In a cinema queue? How does that work?' I was full of curiosity.

'Well,' Mahin continued, 'if a boy is looking for a girl, he typically sends his sister – or female cousin – to look up and down the queue for a pretty girl. She introduces herself to the girl and then subsequently introduces the girl to her brother. Then she acts as chaperone, and they all go into the cinema together. You get the idea?'

'And if a girl is looking for a boy...?'

'Simple, the brother goes looking for a boy and introduces him to his sister. But it's usually the other way around.'

'So, you, Mahin, are breaking the rules?'

'No, not really, we don't break rules. Rules exist to be bent, not broken.'

I stopped eating for a moment and looked at her intently. She looked up. 'Why don't you eat? Why are you looking at me like that?'

My eyes lingered on the red ribbon in her hair.

'I was just thinking… How many hearts have you broken, Mahin?'

A mischievous smile lit up her beautiful face.

'What – men's hearts, you mean?'

'Of course.'

'Why? Lots of them, I guess. Are you surprised?'

'But you're so conceited, callous even.'

'How do you mean, callous, conceited?'

'I mean that you're so very sure of yourself. Don't you give a damn about men's feelings or how much you might hurt them?'

'Look, John,' she continued. 'I know very well from experience that I can sometimes – often, in fact – steal a man's heart just by looking at him in… how shall I say… in a certain way. But it's not fair to blame me for men's weaknesses. Not so long ago, whenever the opportunity arose, I used to look at men like that. It was just for fun. But then I realised that they became jealous and possessive, so I don't do that kind of thing anymore. Besides, as you say, it can be very cruel.'

'Then why are you being cruel to me, Mahin?'

'Me, cruel to you, John? What have I done that you call me cruel?'

I wasn't quite sure how to respond.

She looked at me thoughtfully, pursing her lips. 'You're different.'

'What, blond hair and blue eyes, you mean?'

'That is one example, but it's not just that.'

'Please explain.'

'John, you're so incredibly honest. I find it quite

flattering. I just like sitting listening to you. It's as though you speak to me directly from your heart. It's just so refreshing! I understand perfectly what's going on in your mind.'

I gazed at Mahin in amazement. Her expression appeared impish, mischievous, and she certainly brimmed with confidence. Placing her hand over mine as if to reassure me, she added, 'I really don't want to hurt you.'

She continued eating in silence, whilst I remained motionless. She sensed that I wasn't moving and glanced up.

'Why don't you eat?'

'Mahin, look at me.'

She lifted her head.

'Mahin, I want you to know that I think you have the most beautiful face I've ever seen in my entire life.'

Mahin continues:

I almost choked on my food. To say this was going well would be an understatement. I still felt like I had the upper hand, and that was vital. It would be far too easy to allow myself to be swept away by this man who in truth I had only known a few days. Yet in that time we had revealed so much to each other, and he had been so very open with me. I truly believed he wasn't playing games with me, although I would always have to be wise and retain some mystery. Yet whenever I looked at him, I felt something I had not experienced before. I was so intoxicated by this beautiful man that I found it quite difficult to look at him directly without revealing my feelings.

I carried on eating, but his words 'the most beautiful face I've ever seen' flooded my mind and my heart.

We continued in silence for a few minutes. Both of us had much to think on.

'Mahin, you must have had lots of boyfriends. Tell me about them,' he said.

I was unsure what to say for a moment. No one really compared to John.

'Lots of admirers, for sure, but boyfriends, not so many. Several of my admirers were Americans working in Iran for the US Peace Corps. They were all quite attractive in their own way. Trouble was they were all penniless since they didn't even earn a salary. If they invited me on a date, they expected me to pay the bill. Can you imagine?'

'Did they fall in love with you, Mahin?'

'Oh yes, all my admirers fall in love with me. They can't seem to help themselves. One of them was a university professor, and when he got back home to California, he kept writing me letters asking me to come and live with him there. He said he couldn't get me out of his mind.'

It was good to keep John aware that I was a prize. I certainly had no intentions of being hurt!

John continues:

'How can you tell for sure that a man is in love with you?'

Mahin laughed. 'It's obvious from their behaviour and the things they say.'

'Tell me about one of them, at least.'

'Well, once I had a boyfriend. He was so good looking: tall with beautiful green eyes. He wanted to marry me, but – you won't believe this – he was an Egyptian Jew.'

'An Egyptian Jew? Are there such people?' I asked in disbelief.

'Yes, of course there are. Most of them left Egypt centuries ago when they crossed the Red Sea. Remember the Bible? But they didn't all leave – some remained. His family was one of those. Well, anyway, marrying him was just so complicated we had to give the idea up.'

'You loved him, Mahin?'

'No woman could resist loving such a handsome and charming man. But it was simply hopeless, so we parted. Shall we go?'

Mahin signalled to the waiter that we wanted to leave. But instead of moving, we remained, fixed in one another's gaze. If men make machines for a specific purpose, then God had surely created this woman – the most perfectly fashioned instrument – to rip men's hearts out. I was visibly nervous, transfixed by the red ribbon in her black hair. She had clearly put it there knowing what effect it would have on me. And she was right.

Mahin's huge black eyes burned through mine like lasers. I was shivering in anticipation of something unknown: a subject of forces beyond my control. This stunning woman had possessed me entirely, and I was her captive, willingly enslaved. Was she serious about those blond-haired, blue-eyed children? Or was it just a game she was playing to tease me?

'You'll walk me home?' she asked.

It was a 20-minute walk. We strolled slowly along Aryamehr Avenue arm in arm. It was late. The streets were empty, and there was little traffic. When there was no one around, we would stop under a tree holding hands and just gaze at one another. As Mahin's perfume hypnotised me, I shivered. I became self-conscious and very much aware that she was sensing my state of mind. It was no longer possible to disguise that I was falling in love with her, but I trembled to think that she knew she held my emotions in her grasp.

Eventually we found ourselves under the trees outside her house. She fumbled for the key in her handbag, then slowly opened the iron gate and closed it behind us.

Mahin continues:

We stood there holding hands, alternately embracing and then just gazing at one another. It was unlike any feeling I had had before. As I held him, I thought I would never want to let go, and yet I had to if just to look at him and remind myself just how handsome he was. I wondered if he was aware of how attractive he was. He was tall, several inches taller than me, which was reassuring. But he was so striking. His frequent compliments about my appearance uttered with such sincerity, as well as the striking contrast between us, I found utterly intoxicating. He was unlike any man I had ever known, and I knew at that moment that I would not want to know any other.

I had been trying not to think about that fortune teller and had been sceptical about the words I heard that day.

Yet somehow they had stayed with me. But it terrified me to think that all this may actually be my fate, rather than my free choice. I trembled a little, despite the warm evening air. Even with free choice, I would have chosen John. Yet was it my destiny that caused us to meet, that brought him here in the first place? If so, I would forever be indebted to my fate for choosing such a man for me. And his early experience, of the woman with my complexion who was already married, was merely preparing him for the woman he was destined to be with. For me!

If destiny had chosen to change my life at this point, then I would not fight it. I would accept that this was the man I had been waiting to meet all these years. I held him closer to my body and breathed in his clean masculine scent. I wanted to possess him and to be possessed by him. As all manner of imaginings flashed through my mind, I dared not think on it further. I didn't want to take control at this point: I wanted John to do it for me. Tentatively, my hands explored his body, as if he was my newest possession.

'You feel very tense, John, and your hands are shaking. Is anything the matter?' It was a terrible question really. I knew perfectly well that he felt as I did: terrified and excited simultaneously. To soothe him I placed my hands on either side of his beautiful face and drew him towards me.

John continues:

I was beside myself. Holding Mahin close felt so natural, in a way I had never felt with any woman before. Everything about her was just so extraordinary: her large doe-like eyes, her finely arched brow, her straight nose, her high sculpted cheekbones, her midnight-black hair, her full red lips and pearl-like teeth. Each one of her features was perfect in its own right, but when placed together the effect was exquisite. She was the perfect incarnation of the woman of whom I had always dreamed: my very own Sophia Loren. I couldn't deny it, I was in love. It was a love so vast and so deep I was almost drowning.

There was a moment of perfect silence in this little paradise garden as Mahin held me in her gaze, her breasts lightly grazing my chest. Her perfume heady and intoxicating. I was overcome by an extraordinary sensation: some distant sense of longing and finding. I felt as though all the barriers, real or imaginary, that human beings instinctively erect as defences against others, had suddenly been swept away. I was acutely aware that I was somehow united with Mahin, that some form of conduit had opened between us through which energy was being freely transmitted. We had become one and the same being, and I no longer had any self-control or any need for any self-control. In a state of elation, I felt utterly defenceless. It was as if someone inside me was telling me that without Mahin I would be forever helpless, defenceless. Like a drowning man, my instincts quite suddenly and impulsively took control.

'Mahin, will you marry me?'

There was a pause, utter silence.

'Yes, John, of course I will.'

Mahin continues:

We stood there in shock and elation, staring at each other in disbelief. It was only our third date. I knew John was in love with me. In many ways he had taken me completely by surprise, yet strangely, I had known from the beginning that this would happen. I threw my arms around him, kissed him and held him close. I knew immediately that we had formed an emotional bond that could never be broken. As he held me, I felt profoundly secure; a feeling I hadn't been seeking but that now seemed to complete me. Could this really be true? I buried my fingers in his beautiful hair, the golden hair predicted as part of my destiny. Then I kissed each of his clear blue eyes. The embrace that followed built into a passionate intensity that threatened to slip out of my control. Regaining my composure, I very gently pushed him away.

'It's late. You'd better go now. It's enough for one day. Don't worry, everything will be all right. Call me in the morning.' And after one lingering look, I closed the gate behind him.

John continues:

As I walked back to the villa, I tried to convince myself that I was dreaming. The question I had just asked and the response I had heard were beyond reason or credibility. I had heard the words as I uttered them as if for the first time. I had neither prior knowledge nor intent. It was just 12 days since we had first met at the races. Asking Mahin to marry me was wholly unconsidered – it was as if it had erupted from me. What man with a shred of common sense would ask a girl to marry him without thinking through the consequences first? If anyone had asked me just 10 seconds – five, even – before I proposed whether I was thinking to ask her, I would emphatically and honestly have denied it. There was nothing planned: no ring, no bended knee. My proposal had been utterly unpremeditated. Why? How? It was as though my tongue had taken control of my mind. I walked back in a state of some denial.

And what of Mahin? She accepted my proposal without the least hesitation. Why? Why did she say yes? Was she expecting the question? Or was it as Caroline had explained – Iranians don't say 'no', they tell you what you want to hear? Was Mahin being sincere, or was her answer applied out of kindness like a bandage on an open emotional wound?

I was failing to control a visceral emotion that I should have been able to manage. My emotions appeared to have conquered my reason and common sense, leaving me somewhat disorientated. Should I worry? After all, being in love – yes, I had admitted being in love with Mahin – was a wonderful experience. But did she in turn really love me? I didn't really know; how could I be sure?

As I walked, I began to comfort myself with the thought that such a marriage would never happen in practice. How could it? If she couldn't marry an Egyptian Jew, how could she possibly marry me? Not only were the cultural differences too great, so was the distance – and just about everything else.

On arrival at my accommodation, I changed and climbed into bed. As I closed my eyes, I was overcome by a feeling of having entered an ephemeral paradise. An extraordinary sense of well-being and a profound sense of security seemed to sweep over me: a feeling I hadn't been seeking but now seemed to complete me. With all these conflicting emotions, it was a miracle that I managed to sleep.

9

'GOOGOOSH'

Realise this: one day your soul
will depart from your body and you will
be drawn behind the curtain that floats between us
and the unknown. While you wait for that moment, be happy,
because you don't know where you came from and
you don't know where you will be going.

Omar Khayyam

Mahin:

I lay on my bed, imbued with a feeling of warmth and security that was quite marvellous. I felt that I was drifting above the clouds into a perfect, restful sleep. Later that night my dream descended into a nightmare. Balancing on the edge of an abyss, I could see the fortune teller across the chasm. Her words echoed loudly in my head: 'You will meet a man with blond hair and blue eyes and travel the world.' Now she was standing there knowing that her prediction had come true: I was in love.

But there was a harsh price for this love – she was waiting for me to jump! I could stay safe in my homeland, with my family and friends, or I could choose this man I hardly knew and make a life in a far-off country. I hesitated on the brink, uncertain of my next movement. Suddenly, the figure of John appeared beside her, and my decision was made. It was pre-ordained. I stepped over the precipice.

I jolted awake, shocked and clammy, and my face was wet with tears.

John continues:

Next morning, I awoke in a state of shock; my body was coated in sweat, and my limbs felt frozen. Had I been dreaming? Stretching out my hands, I steadied myself by clutching the steel frames of the bedstead. What had occurred the previous night surely qualified as a victory of emotional intelligence – or rather emotional stupidity – over common sense. 'Dream or nightmare?' I asked myself, breathing deeply to quell my sense of panic. 'Both!' a voice seemed to be saying. Falling in love with a beautiful girl? Yes, a wonderful dream: the work of a seductress *extraordinaire*. I should have been elated, but I was just stunned. Marrying her and all the consequences? Surely a nightmare! My own behaviour seemed inexplicable. I had landed in a foreign country of which I knew next to nothing, and two weeks later I was asking a local girl for her hand in marriage. Again, I spoke aloud: 'Are you mad?' It was a question I couldn't answer.

Years ago, my mother had told me about the Assassin legends: young men seduced by beautiful *houris* before being radicalised and sent off to carry out political assassinations on the instructions of their leader, Hasan-i-Sabah. But those stories were myths and legends. Those poor wretches never got to see their girl again. Believing they would find their *houri* back in paradise, they were destined to commit suicide. But this girl was real – my hands were trembling now – and I was destined to see her again and again: every day until death did us part. I took a deep breath as I tried to grasp the implications of what I had done.

I couldn't relax, so I continued my self-interrogation. Does the unconscious determine everything we do? Was I the victim of natural selection as defined by Darwinian theory, in which dissimilar human beings are attracted to one another? What a wretched trick! This was neither dream nor nightmare, let alone myth or legend. This was reality! Oh, dear God! Small wonder Islamic culture dictates that women should be covered up: to protect not women but men from their own instincts!

Uneasy, I staggered out of bed and stared at my naked body in the mirror. 'John, you idiot! What have you done?' I shuffled into the bathroom. As my hands were still shaking, I thanked whatever powers there may be for my electric razor, or I swear I would have cut myself. Once dressed, I managed gradually to compose myself before going to seek out some breakfast.

'Enjoyable evening, John? Where did you go?'

I still felt jumpy; I almost dropped the jam pot on the floor.

'The Russian Circus at Park-e-Farah.'

'What, you went alone?'

'With a friend,' I added, keeping my tone flat. It would not be wise to elaborate to an office colleague.

'Good show?'

'Oh yes, very impressive. If you've not been, you should try and get to see it.'

After that the subject moved on to more mundane matters, and 45 minutes later, I was sitting behind my office desk wondering what my next move should be. Finally, I plucked up a little courage and called Mahin.

Mahin continues:

I sat for a few minutes at my dressing table. I should have been cleansing my face, but I found myself transfixed by my own reflection. Was I becoming a female Narcissus, in love with my own image? I did feel pleased with myself, satisfied almost to the point of conceit. What a catch: an Englishman proposing to me on just our third date! Unbelievable! Just so romantic. He seemed to have lost control of his senses. Was it luck or destiny? Surely the latter. I hadn't even asked myself if I was truly in love with him. Maybe this is what it felt like when it was meant to be.

That morning I delayed so much that I was very nearly late arriving at the ministry. Hardly had I sat down when my phone rang. I knew it would be him.

'Did you sleep well?'

'Very well, thanks.' I wondered if we were just going to

carry on in this polite vein, when his voice became more urgent.

'What are we going to do, Mahin?'

'Get married. Wasn't that what you asked me?'

John was breathing heavily. 'Yes, but how? Have you told anyone yet, your family?'

'John, first I need a ring, or no one will believe me.'

'Why, yes, of course, of course.' There was another long pause. 'Mahin, I hardly know you; I don't know what came over me last night. It was all so sudden. To be honest I can't begin to believe what happened. Is it really true?'

'Yes. Why do you doubt it?'

'No, I don't doubt it, but I'm having real problems believing it. I don't understand what happened.'

'John, you're in love, that's what happened. You're in love with me and now you're going to marry me.'

Someone knocked at my door. I dropped my voice a little.

'I've got to go. Bye for now!'

As I replaced the receiver, I thought about what he had said. Surely he wasn't having doubts? It was fortunate that I could be resolute enough for both of us.

Later that day Azar rang.

'I want to know all the latest news. Has he proposed to you yet?'

'If you expect me to answer that question, you'll have to promise me faithfully that you'll tell no one.'

'Of course, I promise. Why – has he asked you? I'm desperate to know.'

'Well, as a matter of fact, he has. But it's nothing

serious. A few more weeks and he'll be flying away to Europe, never to return.'

As I heard myself answering Azar, I wondered if I actually meant what I said. Surely I didn't want him to leave?

'But you hardly know him. How did you answer him?'

'I said yes, of course. After all, why should I disappoint him? And besides, I quite enjoy having a young man take me out to various restaurants and nightclubs every few days. So, I immediately gave him the answer he wanted.'

'Honestly, Mahin, you're an opportunist. That's outrageous! Were you surprised he asked?'

'Not really. I understood from the very beginning that he was falling hopelessly in love with me. But it's true, he was very quick. You've no idea the things he says to me.'

'Such as?'

'The very first time we met in the Caspian Hotel, I sat down opposite him, and before I'd hardly said a word, he looked straight at me and said, "Mahin, you're just so beautiful." It's not so much the words he used. I understood immediately he really meant it. It was as though his heart was speaking to me. He's so sincere. I can read his mind just like an open book. I find that really refreshing.'

'And no chaperone?'

'That's the beauty of it: no chaperone!'

'Has he bought you a ring?'

'No, not yet. And I've explained to him that without my father's permission our engagement can't be considered official.'

'So, when's he going to ask your father?'

'He hasn't said. He's got to find the money to buy me a ring first. But honestly, he'll be gone before very long, and that will be that.'

'I'm not so sure. It is exactly as the fortune teller told you. He may well go, but I think he'll come back again, especially if he's really in love with you.'

'Never mind the fortune teller. I told you before, I don't believe all that stuff and nonsense.'

My dreams had clearly told me otherwise, but I didn't want to admit that to Azar yet. Maybe I was still hoping it was all a coincidence?

'Well, I think that you're going to have to believe it. You can't deny that it's all coming true.'

'It certainly has in your case, but in view of what the fortune teller told Tahira, we'd better hope that she was at least partly wrong. I must be getting on with my work now. Now remember, not a word to anyone. You promised.'

It was the next day before John rang to arrange another date.

'John, I'm committed all week, but Thursday evening should be free. Let's meet at the Caspian Hotel and go from there to the Miami Nightclub on the Old Shemiran Road. Googoosh is performing there – she's currently Iran's most iconic pop star. I would love you to see her. She's only 19 and she's fast becoming a symbol of our national pride. It should be an entertaining evening. Please call me again later in the week.'

With that, I terminated the call, yet John remained on my mind for the rest of the day.

John continues:

As time progressed, my feelings about Mahin continued to unsettle me. I was still in a state of denial. It was difficult to acknowledge that I had actually asked her to marry me and that she had accepted. It was simply too much to believe. In fact, the very idea that I might one day go through with marrying Mahin made my blood run cold. It was the practical consequences of such a union that gave me a headache. How would I explain this to my parents and friends when I couldn't even explain it to myself? Lying in bed at night I began to wonder how I might somehow extricate myself. I clearly needed someone to talk to.

The next morning, I tapped on the door to Caroline's office.

'Caroline,' I began awkwardly, 'can you spare me a few minutes?'

'Why, yes, of course, take a seat.'

'You remember last week when I mentioned something about Iranians discussing intimate matters?'

'Yes, I do, and you immediately lied to me, didn't you, John?'

'Am I such a hopeless liar?'

'Absolutely. As an Englishman you don't possess the skills of an Iranian. Now come on, tell me the truth. What's going on?'

'Caroline, just a week after I arrived here, I was introduced to a very beautiful Iranian girl. She rather resembles an Iranian version of Sophia Loren.'

'That beautiful?'

'Even more beautiful, in my opinion.'

'Goodness gracious!'

'We went out a couple of times, once to a restaurant and then on a picnic trip over the mountains with her brother and his girlfriend. Then on our third date we went to the Russian Circus, then a restaurant afterwards. I walked her home, and when we arrived, she invited me in just behind her garden gate. Caroline, this girl is just so stunning. My heart was missing beats. Well, you may imagine what happened.'

Caroline sat upright in her chair. 'You kissed her?'

'But that wasn't all.'

'What else did you do to her?' Caroline asked, sounding alarmed.

'I don't think it was what I did to her but rather what she did to me.'

'Good heavens, John, my imagination is at bursting point. What did she do?'

'It's very hard to explain – or at least to explain in words that you might actually believe. Once behind the gate, as we embraced, I began shaking all over as though I was possessed somehow, and all of a sudden I asked her to marry me.'

'To marry you? After just three dates? You're joking! And how did she reply?'

'She accepted.'

'What, just like that?'

'Yes. I know it's unbelievable, and after I'd left her a little while later, I kept telling myself that it wasn't true. I was in complete denial. I mean, can you imagine? I asked her simply on impulse, unpremeditatedly, without any thought of the consequences. I must have been out of my mind.'

'I don't believe what I'm hearing. Who is she, for heaven's sake?'

'She's secretary to the minister of agriculture.'

'What, personal secretary?'

'Oh yes, the ministry even provides a chauffeur-driven car to take her to the ministry offices every day.'

'What's her name?'

'Mahin Rashvand, and she claims that her ancestors were the legendary Assassins of Alamut.'

'Are you in love with her? I suppose you must be. What are you going to do?'

'That's what I've come to ask you. On the one hand I must admit that yes, I'm in love with her. I make no excuses for that. But on the other hand, I'm terrified. I want to run away.'

'Well, that's what you're going to do, surely? Once your replacement arrives, you'll be gone. So, where's the worry?'

'That's just it, Caroline. How am I going to get this girl out of my mind? She's driving me crazy. Every time I see her, I feel like a mess of testosterone and adrenaline. She's just so stunning.'

'Goodness! Where did you meet her?'

'Almost three weeks ago at the races. She was sitting just behind me on the tribunes. When her American friend asked to borrow my programme and invited me up to sit between them, I felt as though I was sitting next to Sophia Loren. But it's too complicated! I think I'm going to try and brush her off. I'm petrified. I'm seriously horrified. The trouble is I'm not sure I've the strength to do it. Being all alone here in Tehran, with no one to turn to, I've come to you for moral support.'

Caroline smiled at me.

'Well, it's very early days. I'm sure something will happen soon enough leading to a disagreement – it always does. Once that happens, you will have an excuse to leave. Let it happen naturally. I don't know what else to suggest.'

I stood up to leave. 'Thanks, Caroline.'

'Good luck and do please tell me how you get on.'

The following Thursday evening I was again waiting for Mahin in the reception hall of the Caspian Hotel. She walked in looking absolutely stunning in a knee-length pink cocktail dress with silver embroidery around the neck and hem, a tight-fitting embroidered belt and silver high-heeled shoes and earrings.

'You look fabulous. I think you've been shopping again,' I exclaimed, leaning forward to kiss her on both cheeks.

To my surprise Mahin recoiled from my advance. 'I've just come from the hairdressers, and John, please refrain from kissing me in public. It's unacceptable for men and women to kiss in public in Iran.'

Suitably chastised, I called the waiter to take an order for drinks.

As we waited for the drinks to come, I must have been staring at her.

'What are you looking at?'

'You, of course. Are you really going to marry me?'

'I've a reputation for not changing my mind, and if you want to change yours, then I think you should remember that it's not for us human beings to decide who we fall in love with. If you're really in love with me as much as you say you are, and my heart is telling me that it's true, then falling out of love again could be quite problematic. We humans are subject to no greater force than that of our emotions. They're bigger and more powerful than we are.'

She seemed to be watching me to see how I would reply, but I looked away, unsure. I felt she could see into my mind, and all my doubts were laid bare in there. She stretched her hand out to mine in reassurance – only letting go when the waiter arrived with the drinks.

For a moment it was just too much. I couldn't meet her gaze, so I looked at the wall beyond.

'I don't know how we're going to do it. We are living thousands of miles apart. We come from very different cultures. I don't understand a word of your language, and I can't for the life of me imagine how we can arrange a wedding. Maybe we should get married in England. What do you think?'

I looked at Mahin.

'That's out of the question. My father would never agree. He would never let me leave Iran in the hands of a stranger to live in another country.' Mahin paused. 'Besides, what's the hurry? I intend to finish my university education before I marry.'

'When will that be?'

'Another year. Maybe by then you can find a job in Iran and come and live here. Then we could marry sooner, and we could live in my house together. That would be wonderful.'

I looked at Mahin intently for a moment and imagined myself living with her in her own house. The idea seemed irresistible.

'But I've only just started a new job in Switzerland. I can't just walk away, and besides, I have no idea how or where I might find a job in Iran,' I replied.

'John, I think we're going too fast. Let's slow down. Let's enjoy this evening, and besides, as you say, we hardly know one another.'

It was a relief to change the subject.

'How far is the Miami Nightclub from here? Can we walk or do we need a taxi?'

Mahin looked at her watch. 'If we leave soon, we can walk.'

I called for the bill and we got up to leave.

The Miami Nightclub consisted essentially of a curved stage surrounded by about 30 circular tables of varying diameters. The first thing that struck me as we sat down was that most of the tables had been taken by Arabs dressed in their white robes.

'What are they all doing here?'

Mahin smiled. 'They are here for a weekend away from their wives and their own regulations. Both of which severely restrict nightlife in their own countries. Besides, Googoosh has quite a reputation all over the Middle East, and they want to see her.'

By the time we had placed our order and begun to eat, the club was filled to capacity. At nine o'clock the curtains opened to reveal a small orchestra. Moments later Googoosh appeared on stage dressed in a tight-fitting, full-length red dress. She seemed very young. Her face was round, and like most Iranian girls, her hair was black. She bowed and addressed the audience. I didn't understand a word she was saying, and nor, I supposed, did all the Arab clients.

The orchestra struck up, and Googoosh began singing. I had just turned my chair for a better view when I was stunned by a violent scream in my left ear. Googoosh looked straight at me, her voice faltering as she did so. For an instant I failed to understand what had happened, and then to my great embarrassment I realised that every Arab in the club was also staring at me. I felt my face redden. I didn't know which way to look. Then after what seemed like eternity Googoosh resumed singing. I turned to look at Mahin, who was smiling.

'Surely that wasn't you?'

'Yes, of course it was.'

'What on earth? What did you shout?'

'I shouted that she should sing louder.'

'Unbelievable. I've never felt so embarrassed in my entire life,' I replied, the indignation clear in my voice.

Mahin scowled at me in disgust. 'What the hell, we're paying a lot of money to come here and listen to her. She was singing much too quietly. I want to be entertained, not just whispered at. Besides, given that there's hardly anyone else in here who speaks Farsi, who's going to correct her?'

The atmosphere between us remained glacial for the rest of the evening. I was mortified. We sat in silence listening to Googoosh whilst ignoring one another. As soon as we had finished eating, Mahin stood up. 'Let's go.'

I settled up and we made our way out into the street, but still no words passed between us. Having hailed a taxi, I opened the door for Mahin, and as soon as she sat down and I was about to close it, she turned on me.

'You asked me to marry you, an offer I accepted, and now you do this to me. I learned at school that an Englishman's word is his bond. Now I know the truth. It's worthless!'

'Better a broken bond than a broken marriage,' I yelled, slamming the taxi door.

Walking home, I felt a great sense of relief. Maybe my life could return to normal.

The next day was a Friday, and the office was closed. I rose late and prepared myself a leisurely breakfast of bacon and eggs and then sat at the table to write a letter home. I wrote in much detail about recent events but omitted to mention anything about my Iranian girlfriend.

Every Saturday morning – Saturday being the first day of the week – a team meeting was held in the architects' offices to discuss progress and plan the forthcoming week's priorities. On this occasion I had been asked to present my first report on anticipated outturn costs for the project. The structural design for the leaning towers had become extremely challenging. The steel sections required to support them could not be fabricated in Iran since steel production was limited to quite small sections commonly used in relatively simple buildings. They would therefore need to be imported by sea, unloaded at the Port of

Khorramshahr on the Persian Gulf and brought to Tehran either by road or by rail. Initial estimates indicated that the sections would be too large for transportation through some of the curved tunnels on the Trans-Iranian Railway, while if they were transported by road, numerous bridges might need to be strengthened between Khorramshahr and Tehran, the costs of which were unknown and could be considerable.

Unsurprisingly these matters were discussed at length during the meeting. Whilst I was being interrogated about the cost implications, a receptionist came in saying that she had a lady on the telephone who wished to speak to me urgently.

'Who is it?'

'She didn't say.'

'Take her name and number and tell her I'll call her back as soon as I've finished here.'

The meeting resumed, only to be interrupted almost immediately by the same receptionist. The lady on the telephone couldn't wait; her call was extremely urgent. Before I could reply, the receptionist turned on her heel, declaring, 'I'll put her through right now.'

I was furious. I didn't need to guess who it might be. While waiting for the phone to ring, all the participants began talking among themselves. I had been working on the project for more than a month now, and for me this was the first meeting of any significance. *Has she got spies in here? Has she bribed the receptionist? Will this woman stop at nothing?* I thought.

The phone rang, and I picked up the receiver.

'Hello?'

'John, it's Mahin. I must see you tonight.'

'Look, Mahin, it's all over. I don't want to see you again.'

'But you know I love you!'

I paused. Now she says it! Really?

I needed to bring the conversation to an end. 'Yes, I love you too, but it's just impossible. We can't go any further. I can't talk. I'm in a meeting.'

There was a silence in the room, and all eyes were on me. I felt my cheeks redden. How unprofessional this appeared to be. How could I get her off the phone?

'All right then – six o'clock in the Caspian Hotel,' I whispered.

'No, not there. Seven o'clock in front of the Roudaki Hall. Fereydoon has invited us to a concert, and I have the tickets,' Mahin replied triumphantly.

'OK, see you then.'

I hung up – eyebrows were raised in curiosity as the meeting resumed. Later that day I passed Caroline in the office corridor.

'The gossip is all around the office, John. What a woman. Talk about persistent – she almost reduced the receptionist to tears! It's all over then?'

'Hopefully it will be after I fly back to Switzerland at the end of the month. Last night we went out to the Miami Nightclub to listen to Googoosh. We had an argument, and I broke off the engagement. She was most indignant, but quite frankly I was quite relieved because the whole affair was really getting me stressed out. After last night I thought it was all over. That was until she rang today. You heard what happened. She's such a strong character. When she wants something, she will let nothing stand in her way until she succeeds in getting it.'

'It's obvious to me that she's in love with you, John. How serious was the argument?'

'It was about her inappropriate behaviour. We were listening to the singing, and suddenly she shouted at Googoosh at the top of her voice to sing louder. Googoosh faltered, and seconds later the entire audience – mostly Arabs – was looking at our table. It was just so embarrassing.'

Caroline laughed. 'If you choose to have Iranian friends, then differences in culture and unconventional behaviour are part of the package – and don't I know it. I shouldn't bother to be upset by an incident like that. If Googoosh wasn't singing loud enough, your girlfriend probably considered she wasn't worth the money – hence her intervention. She really must be quite a character.'

'I suppose you're probably right.'

'So, you're seeing her again?'

'I really don't know what to do. What do you think?'

'Well, if she's as beautiful as you say, and you really are in love with her, then why not? But if that phone call this morning is anything to go by, then in my view, she has no intention of letting you go.'

'In a few weeks I'll be going anyway. So, for the little time I have left I suppose I might as well continue seeing her.'

'Good luck, and please bring me a photo of this girl. I'm seriously curious. Must go!' And with that, Caroline disappeared down the corridor.

By the time I reached the steps of the Roudaki Hall, Mahin was standing awaiting my arrival with a broad smile on her face. She slipped her arm through mine as we climbed the steps, and we found our way down to the front of the impressive auditorium. Remarkably, she made no mention of the events the previous Thursday evening. It was as though the incident had never happened.

Mahin continues:

Fortunately, John appeared to be over his ridiculous overreaction. He clearly needed more exposure to our culture and how we behave. We certainly do not put up with less than perfect service, and why should we? Anyway, he would soon put it behind him when he saw the splendours of the Roudaki Hall. This beautiful building had been designed by an Iranian-American architect in the style of the Vienna State Opera and inaugurated less than two years earlier during the festivities of the shah's coronation. The hall was named after a blind Persian poet of the ninth and tenth centuries, Abu-Abdollāh Roudaki, and the building is now among the best-equipped and most modern opera houses in the world. The auditorium seats 12 hundred, excluding two tiers of boxes and balconies. I was pleased to note that he looked around with some awe.

'What are we going to see tonight?'

I opened my programme. 'First of all, there will be some Iranian classical music followed by some dances performed by members of the Bakhtiari tribes from the province of Fars. They have very colourful costumes.

Then there will be some vocalists singing Iranian classical songs, and finally after the interval the orchestra will play Mozart's *Eine Kleine Nachtmusik*.'

I settled back into my seat, happy that John had recovered from his previous mood.

John continues:

'That sounds wonderful. I'm really looking forward to it.'

At first, I found the Iranian classical music rather strange, but gradually I developed an appreciation. The folk dances were highly entertaining, with lots of Bakhtiari girls in their full-length colourful red dresses.

Mahin never missed an opportunity to stress the limits of Islamic influence. 'You see, these tribes never wear any kind of veil. They traditionally spend the summer months high in the Zagros Mountains of south-west Persia with their flocks, where the influence of Islam is almost negligible. Until recently their lives had not changed since the days of the Achaemenid Empire.'

'And in the winter?' I asked.

'They migrate en masse, thousands and thousands of them, with their flocks of sheep and goats from the province of Fars to the province of Khuzestan. I have never witnessed it, but these people are so hardy and so self-sufficient. It's an incredible sight to behold.'

Whilst it was good that we seemed to have moved on from our unpleasant end to the previous evening, I did feel I should make some reference to it.

'You seem quite unconcerned about our argument the other night,' I ventured.

Mahin turned and looked straight at me. 'Why should I be concerned if you don't mind being cheated? Why go into a nightclub and pay good money for mediocre entertainment? I shouted at Googoosh in your interest, and yet you blame me for upsetting you. I don't see the logic in that. How else could I put her right? By throwing my plate at her?' Indignant, she turned back to look at the stage.

I was speechless; yet again she had made her point very forcefully. It was almost humiliating. The atmosphere eased as she fell into conversation with the lady seated to her left. Obviously, I was excluded by the language.

After the interval I enjoyed the more familiar melodies of Mozart, in which Fereydoon played lead violin.

Following the performance Fereydoon and Mahdokht joined us for dinner in a nearby restaurant. Fereydoon, who was sitting next to his girlfriend and opposite me and Mahin, was anxious to know my impressions.

'My impressions are very positive,' I replied. 'I was fascinated by the instruments used for the Iranian folksongs – they were quite unfamiliar – and the haunting soulful lilt of the singers' voices. Reflective of a deep, colourful and ancient culture, I imagine. Although I must ask why Iranian songs so often sound sad?'

Mahdokht's black eyes stared into mine, and in broken English she offered her own explanation. 'So much of Iranian history is about war and invasions, and our people have suffered so much for so many centuries, and that makes for so many broken hearts.'

'That's true,' Fereydoon added, 'but we do have happy songs as well.'

After that the conversation went into Farsi, and I was lost in my own thoughts. When the bill arrived, Fereydoon and I settled in cash, and we walked along the road to where he had parked his car. Geography dictated that I would be dropped off first and the girls afterwards. It was late, and soon enough we reached my destination. Just before I alighted onto the pavement, Mahin placed her hands behind my neck and, grasping me firmly, kissed each of my eyelids in turn. Seconds later Fereydoon's car, with its precious cargo, turned the corner and disappeared into the night.

The following Thursday afternoon we went to see the crown jewels in the vaults of the central bank in Firdausi Avenue – the so-called Jewellery Museum. Mahin managed to locate an English-speaking guide, who began by explaining that what we were about to see was the largest and most dazzling collection of jewellery in state ownership in the entire world.

Once inside the museum I gasped. There were buckets full of precious stones all around the hall, arranged like an Aladdin's cave. In the centre was a golden globe representing the earth, which the guide explained was made of 35 kilograms of pure gold and on which were mounted no fewer than 51,366 pieces of jewellery. The globe on its diamond-encrusted stand was 110 centimetres high and 45 centimetres in diameter. The oceans were covered in emeralds and the land areas in rubies, while the latitudes and longitudes were picked out in diamonds. Interestingly, Iran and Britain, in view of their importance, had a special diamond each. The guide explained that the globe dated from the Qajar dynasty in the 19th century.

Next, we looked at the so-called Peacock Throne. The guide explained that a significant quantity of the Iranian Crown Jewels was brought to Iran by Nader Shah following his military exploits in India in the 18th century, when he sacked the cities of Delhi and Agra. When he was assassinated a few years later, the Peacock Throne was either lost or destroyed, and this throne was the one subsequently reconstructed by Fath-Ali Shah Qajar in the 19th century. Its proper name was the Sun Throne, but it has since been erroneously referred to as the Peacock Throne, a term used in the West as a metonym for the Iranian monarchy.

I turned to our guide, 'Am I right in thinking that somewhere in this museum is the largest diamond in the world?'

She led us over to look at the famous *Daryayeh-i-Nur*, the 'Sea of Light', the largest uncut diamond in the world. 'This is the sister of the *Kuh-i-Nur* or "Mountain of Light", the largest cut diamond in the world, which today can be seen in the Tower of London.'

'How did that end up in the Tower of London?'

'That's a long and complicated story, but briefly, it found its way back to India and into the hands of the East India Company, whose officers presented it to Queen Victoria.'

Then we came to the Pahlavi crown, beset with 3,380 diamonds, 369 natural pearls and five emeralds, and the

Shahi Sword with its three thousand stones. But what caught my eye were the tiaras and necklaces worn by the empress Farah at her coronation a few years before. One tiara she had worn for her wedding 10 years earlier boasted one of the largest pink diamonds in the world, but most breathtaking of all were the tiara and necklace, with huge green emeralds surrounded with diamonds.

The guide, who was watching us admiring them, smiled. Pointing to the tiaras worn by the shah's two sisters, she asked, 'Do you know that "tiara" is a Greek word for a Persian headdress?'

Mahin looked at them longingly. 'They look quite dazzling when our empress wears them.'

I turned and looked at Mahin. 'I think that they would look at least as beautiful adorning you.'

10

TALES OF THE ASSASSINS

It's too bad if a heart lacks fire,
and is deprived of the light
of a heart ablaze.
The day on which you are
without passionate love
is the most wasted day of your life.

Omar Khayyam

John:

A week later I arranged to meet Mahin in the Xanadu Restaurant, where I had become a frequent visitor. I phoned in advance to reserve an intimate table for two in a quiet corner of the garden. I was becoming increasingly obsessed with the idea that I was in love with a descendant of the famous medieval Assassins. It would explain the spell her beauty had cast over me; I had surely been bewitched by my very own *houri* from paradise? More than ever, I wanted to know all about these infamous people. Mahin had promised to explain everything to me over a dish of pepper steak.

When I arrived soon after seven, there was the usual row of expatriates drinking beer at the bar. I was grateful to occupy the one remaining bar stool in the homely surroundings of this delightful establishment. The Russian owner was regaling her regular clients with drinks, and when she saw me, she placed a glass of beer on the bar and declared, 'A table for two, then; you have company tonight?'

'Yes,' I replied, 'I do.'

'Is she charming?' she added, her eyes twinkling.

'Yes, very charming indeed.'

Some 30 minutes later Mahin appeared. Heads turned, and she immediately became the cynosure of all male eyes. I leapt to my feet to welcome her, and as I did so, all the other fellows stood up also, each hopefully offering her his own stool. Our Russian hostess watched this performance with evident delight, and Mahin was soon sitting on her chosen stool and accepting my offer of a small glass of cold beer.

Shortly afterwards a waiter appeared with menus advising us that our table was ready outside. Mahin duly installed herself in the corner of the walled garden, where she had a clear view of the fountain and all the other clients. As for me, I was delighted to be undistracted and able to focus all my attention on my lover with her back to the wall. We both ordered jumbo-sized deep-fried Persian Gulf prawns followed by pepper steak.

'Now,' I began, 'I want to know all about those ancestors of yours, the Assassins of Alamut. I'm fascinated. Who were they and where did they come from?'

Mahin continues:

John seemed so animated tonight; he was certainly captivated by this topic. It was fortunate that I had much to tell him.

'First of all, in Farsi we don't call them Assassins; we call them Ismailis. The word *Assassin* comes from the Arabic word *hashish*, meaning *herbage* or *greens* or, as you surely know, a potent drug. In Farsi the word *assass* means *foundation,* both in a physical as well as in a virtual sense.'

'So, who then were the Ismailis?' John asked somewhat impatiently.

'A Shia religious sect. When the Prophet Mohammad died, he left no will, and almost immediately a dispute broke out over the succession whether the leader of the Muslims should thereafter be determined by election or by dynastic succession. In the event, the Prophet's most senior companion, Abu Bakr, was elected initially as caliph, sidelining the Prophet's cousin and son-in-law, Ali. Those who became known as the Sunni branch of Islam favoured an electoral process, disavowing the dynastic principle favoured by the Shia. It's a bitter and complicated schism that continues to this day, but the point here is that following the deaths of the Prophet's other senior companions, Abu Bakr and Omar, who in turn were also elected caliphs, Ali succeeded them, becoming – in the Shia tradition – the first of 12 imams. Imam Jaffar, the sixth imam, had two sons Ismail and Musa al-Kazem. The Ismailis – also known as the Seveners – believe Ismail to be the seventh and last imam, whereas the so-called

Twelvers believe the descendants of Musa al-Kazem to be the rightful imams.'

I could see John gazing at me quizzically.

'Do you really want me to continue with this unromantic discussion?' I asked. Much to my relief, the prawns arrived, allowing me time to calculate the different calendars.

'In the 11th century the Seljuk Turks invaded Iran and progressively established a vast empire stretching from the Hindu Kush in the east to Anatolia in the west, including most of Syria and Palestine.'

'Where did the Turks come from?'

'Well certainly not from Turkey, if that was what you imagined. They came from their homelands near the Aral Sea, east of the Caspian. Moreover, being Sunnis, they considered one of their primary roles to be the defence of Sunni Islam against its greatest threats the invasion of the European Crusaders in Syria as well as the very real threat of what they perceived as the treacherous and highly ambitious Ismailis.'

'And Hasan-i-Sabah?' John asked.

'Hasan was brought up in a traditional Twelver Shia family not far from Tehran, but as a young man he developed an interest in learning all about the Islamic faith, and in time he became so impressed by the superior intellectual aspects of Ismaili beliefs that he eventually became their de facto leader in Iran. There are many stories about Hasan-i-Sabah and it is difficult to distinguish fact from fiction. One such story is that at some point Hasan went through an intellectual crisis and fell seriously ill, and as the story goes, when he recovered, he thought he was someone else. Although it is contested, Hasan began questioning the very existence of God, and having read all the holy books, he reached the blasphemous conclusion that they were mostly fairy stories and fabrications written by persons with unbalanced minds. He became convinced that it was impossible to prove the existence or otherwise of God, indeed that His existence was unknowable. So, he went out into the streets and began preaching that God didn't exist and that the predicted return of Jesus Christ and the Twelfth Imam was just a hollow promise. The people were troubled and began throwing stones at him, until some other mullahs reproached him, telling him to stop, adding that the people needed something tangible, some beliefs to hold on to. Besides, if they did not believe in – and fear – God, there would be anarchy in the land, and worse still, the clergy would be unemployed. So, realising they had a valid point of view, he reluctantly stopped.'

The waiter arrived to take our plates, and I paused. But John was still animated and wanted to discuss it further.

'Is that what you believe, Mahin? Are you convinced that the clergy don't, in their heart of hearts, believe in God?'

I smiled at John's question. 'The simple ones may be devout believers, and certainly none would dare deny believing in God, but personally I'm convinced that most of them don't believe a word of it. On the other hand, people are entitled to believe whatever they like. Undoubtedly, believing in God and life after death gives some people a sense of security. But everyone needs to earn money, and for the clergy, convincing people to believe in God is an excellent form of business.'

As our steak arrived, John challenged me. 'You're a real atheist then?'

'Of course!' I continued, 'The mullahs may appear crazy, but they're not stupid; they're businesspeople like everyone else. Most of them love money.' I took a mouthful of steak. John did likewise and stared straight into my eyes as he savoured his meat. 'Haven't you heard enough yet?' I asked.

'No, absolutely not. I really want to understand this Hasan fellow. Mahin, please continue.'

'Hasan was very concerned about the dreadful consequences of the oppressive behaviour of the Turks on the indigenous Iranian population and began developing a plan to start a rebellion. Realising he could not possibly defeat the Seljuks on an open battleground, he came up with a cunning strategy based on fortification, infiltration and assassination. If the people were so stupid as to believe in God and the promise of paradise in the next life, he surmised, then they could be persuaded to believe in almost anything. And so it was that Hasan developed, and for the first time unsheathed, what we Iranians call the "Shia weapon". He began converting the largely Sunni Persian population to Shiism with the deliberate intention of exploiting the Sunni–Shia schism in Islam to justify a war of attrition against the occupying Sunni Turks. After many years spent preaching to the masses, he arrived in Ghazvin and subsequently seized the fortress of Alamut, high in the Alborz mountains, where he began instructing and training his fanatical, radicalised Shia recruits in the art of political assassination. According to legend he never came down from Alamut until his death some 35 years later.'

John continues:

'I must let you finish your steak, but there are so many things I want to understand. For instance, is it true that Hasan killed his own son for drinking wine? Surely, if Hasan himself didn't believe in God, he would never have done such a terrible thing? Most of all I want to know all about those gorgeous *houris* in his garden of paradise. Where did they come from?'

Mahin looked up from her plate and smiled, a knowing smile as if to imply that I was looking at the answer to my own question. I stared straight into the black pupils of her almond-shaped eyes and, returning her smile, raised my glass to toast.

Mahin continues:

'You must understand that if someone decides to justify their actions based on either a theory or even a lie – and in this instance, I mean believing in God and the sayings of his prophets – then that someone must never do, or say, anything that exposes that lie for what it really is. If the rules say that alcohol is forbidden, then there can be no exceptions. So yes, I can easily believe that Hasan had his own son murdered for drinking wine.'

John raised his wine glass and gulped. 'But, Mahin, in

the eyes of true believers, what you have just said is an absolute heresy!'

'Yes, of course it is. But unless you understand and accept what I have just explained, you will never understand the politics of my country, or I suspect, centuries ago, the politics of yours either. Let me move on. Hasan-i-Sabah convinced his followers that he was not just their leader but God's representative on Earth, with the power to decide who goes to heaven or hell. This was the central tenet of his strategy. These beliefs were the instrument that enabled him to wage a war of attrition against the Seljuk Turks carried out by means of political assassinations. From a moral standpoint, he justified this strategy on the grounds that his method of fighting the Turks would involve a lesser loss of life than a full-scale war. Those of his followers who succeeded in their bloodthirsty missions had first to be persuaded beyond any shadow of doubt that they would be rewarded in paradise and received into the arms of the most beautiful *houris*. Hasan was an extraordinarily talented man. He effectively established a state within a state stretching from Syria in the west to the border of China in the east. The Seljuk Turks, despite numerous attempts, failed to eradicate the Ismailis. It was almost 200 years later when they were finally defeated by the Mongols, in the 13th century. The Ismailis are credited with having constructed as many as 250 mountain fortresses. The Mongols recorded having found a plaque at Alamut inscribed with the names of as many as 50 Assassins and their victims. Don't you see, Hasan was a national hero!'

John continues:

Mahin's steak must have been almost cold by now. We sat in silence until she had finished, and then we ordered our desserts. As I sat watching her and savouring my wine, my imagination blazed. I was looking for confirmation that I was in love with a descendant of one of Hasan's *houris*. It had to be true. Surely this woman sitting opposite me was a reincarnation of one of Hasan's honeytraps, a living lethal weapon whose sole purpose was to steal the hearts of men? That very thought was as terrifying as it was intriguing, and I relished it as much as my pepper steak.

My look of expectation encouraged her to continue.

'I don't know what to tell you about the gardens of paradise. They certainly could not have been located at Alamut itself; there's no space for them on the peak of that isolated mountain and little water for their irrigation. There may be some truth about the drugging of Hasan's followers with hashish. But all those stories about *houris* and gardens were surely legends made up by Marco Polo or the people he met on his travels. In any event the Ismailis were Iranians just like I am. I doubt we have changed much down the centuries, so you can believe what you like.'

I found Mahin's explanation about the gardens of paradise something of a disappointment. We sat chatting for a while, savouring our desserts; then, having settled the bill, we waved goodbye to our Russian hostess. We took a taxi to Aryamehr Avenue. Outside her garden gate,

Mahin slipped her hand into her handbag before turning the lock with her key.

Once inside, she took my hands in hers, and as we moved closer, her breasts grazed me lightly and her perfume filled my senses. Then she took a small step backwards and fixed me with her gaze.

Mahin continues:

'You asked me about Hasan's *houris*. Now look into my eyes and imagine for a moment that you are one of Hasan's followers and for the first time in your life you are looking at the woman of your dreams, that in your perception she is a model of perfect human beauty – the shape of her face, the outline of her nose, her immaculate complexion, the form of her high cheekbones, the line of her jaw, the shape of her lips, her perfect row of white teeth, her inviting smile and, most beautiful of all, her big black eyes. Her silken hair falls to her shoulders. Imagine that she is the perfect incarnation of the most enticing creature you've ever imagined. She is dressed in the finest silk. The most ornate jewellery hangs from her neck and her ears, made from sapphires, diamonds and amethysts. Adorning her head is a sparkling tiara of diamonds and green emeralds. As you get closer, you are intoxicated by her perfume. How would you feel?'

John hesitated for a moment.

'I would feel precisely what I'm feeling now, Mahin, my head spinning, my emotions in turmoil, and overcome by fear of having to admit that I'm in love.'

John's eyes glistened with tears.

'Fear? Fear of what, John?'

'Fear that my judgement will be compromised by my emotions. Horror – that I'm in a love so vast and so deep that I'm drowning in it.'

I placed my hand on John's forehead.

'You're very hot…'

'Mahin, I'm on fire! I'm burning with passion!'

I felt my body jolt as John pulled me close to him. I admit to being thrilled by clear evidence of his desire. I felt moved, less in control than I was used to. In that moment I was ready to yield to the thrill of knowing that I was loved deeply in return. Men had claimed to love me before, and many had hoped to win my affections, but this was different. Previously, I was secure in my reserve, my self-control. Was I ready to accept that this was my destiny? Whilst bathing in the discovery of my readiness to accept John, I also knew that I must retain my mystery. Those visceral feelings were my secret and mine alone. I must keep my composure; I must not under any circumstances reveal any weakness. I must be strong. Yet this intensity was in danger of overwhelming me. I confess I had dreamed since puberty of having a man with blond hair and blue eyes for a lover, but I must guard these inner desires. While I determined to keep my innermost feelings to myself, I actively sought to persuade John to admit his undying love for me. I must test him. I pushed him gently away and smiled at him, a smile that would burn right through his heart. His reactions reassured me his emotions and his heart were firmly in my grasp. The feeling of security I drew from that was heady and satisfying.

'Why do you fight with yourself? Just give in and accept the reality that you cannot fight a power that is bigger and stronger than you are. Then you will find bliss and peace and share it with me,' I said.

'I'm too frightened!' John's eyes were watering now, the tears running down his cheeks. He was breaking down like a child, and I could see that he hated himself for it, but he simply could not hold back any longer. I paused. For a moment my heart ached for him. I knew I was deliberately playing with his emotions to the point of cruelty. But he would have to defend himself. I couldn't and shouldn't do that for him.

'You don't know how lucky you are. Just imagine, had we not met at the races just three weeks ago, what would you be doing on a Friday afternoon? Sitting in your room, drinking beer and playing cards with yourself to pass the time? Unlike those Fedayeen who were tricked by Hasan-i-Sabah, you are not in heaven or hell. You are still in the real world – with me!'

John continues:

'Mahin, you wonder why I'm terrified. I admit and accept that I'm in love with you, and it's true that not many days ago I impulsively asked you to marry me. But either that was an expression of profound emotion or I was out of my mind. I made that proposal without a moment's reflection. It didn't even occur to me to get down on bended knee as tradition requires. It just erupted from inside me as though someone else was asking.'

Mahin continues:

'Perhaps someone was! But whatever the reason, I knew that it came from the very depths of your heart. I knew from that first moment that you were the man I saw in my dreams many years ago. I have been waiting for you all this time, and for that reason I accepted without a moment's hesitation.'

'But isn't it ridiculous? Beyond being in love, we have nothing in common; we're like chalk and cheese.'

'John, in exchange for your love, I'm willing to follow you wherever you go.'

'You mean... give up your country, your job, your house, your friends, your family...'

'Well, I would like to complete my studies first, but yes, John, for you, yes. Now kiss me again.'

As I released myself from John's passionate kiss, I pushed him gently away, and while holding him firmly by my left hand, I stretched out my right hand to touch the garden wall. With my index finger, I traced an invisible cross.

'John, look, I've marked my garden wall with a cross. Swear you will return.' I paused and fixed him in my gaze.

John continues:

I could feel my heart racing. I flinched but couldn't answer – my tongue felt swollen, paralysed in my mouth. This trance of desire tossed me between agony and ecstasy with each breath. Mahin could clearly sense the ardour running through my body as she held me close and pressed herself firmly against me. Then, raising her slender arms, she ran her fingers through my hair, caressing my head as she did so.

'You're mine, John. There's no other way. But it's better you go now.' She turned as if to walk away from me, before looking up towards her balcony. Smiling, she whispered into my ear. 'Come back later in the year and marry me, and I'll take you upstairs. Then you can have your *houri* in paradise.'

11

HOW TO DRIVE A BARGAIN

Dead yesterdays and unborn tomorrows,
why fret about it, if today be sweet?

Omar Khayyam

John:

A few days later I received news that Harry would soon be returning to Tehran accompanied by my permanent replacement.

The following Friday morning Mahin asked me to go with her to the bazaar, where she intended buying a carpet. As soon as I had finished my breakfast, I walked to her house, rang the bell and waited for her to join me in the street outside before going to find a taxi.

'The bazaar is located right in the south of the city near the railway station. In the heavy traffic it will take at least half an hour to get there,' Mahin explained.

Some 10 minutes later we found two seats in the back of an already crowded taxi. Mahin was still bargaining the price as it moved off. I had become used to this extraordinary procedure – if Mahin refused to accept the fare demanded by the driver, he would stop the taxi and she would get out, dragging me behind her. It was all a bluff, but it was very stressful. The inconvenienced other passengers would try to complain but would be ignored, while the traffic held up behind the taxi would honk their horns in protest. It was utterly deafening, but Mahin would not be ruffled; she would simply take her time and invariably get her way. As she always did.

It was now the middle of June, and the heat of the sun was unrelenting, mitigated only marginally by the shade of the trees in Pahlavi Avenue. The further downhill we went, the hotter it became and the slower the taxi progressed. This one was an old Mercedes-Benz that, if the meter was still working, had more than three hundred thousand kilometres on the clock. When we reached Shah Reza Avenue, the driver turned a sharp left and straight into the oncoming traffic. The technique for such a manoeuvre was always the same: precipitously turn and propel the taxi through the smallest space between two oncoming vehicles. This navigation was executed regardless of possible consequences and was accompanied by another cacophony of protest.

'No wonder the whole world is in such a mess,' I exclaimed.

'Why?' Mahin sounded surprised.

'Because God has a full-time job here taking care of these crazy drivers and their passengers.'

Mahin laughed and translated for the driver, who by

then was going headlong into the next line of traffic. He just shrugged, while the other passengers looked at me in amusement. Minutes later we turned right down Ferdowsi Avenue. This avenue was named after the famous Persian poet who was immortalised in the form of a large statue, sitting cross-legged on a plinth, at the upper end of the avenue. The taxi was barely moving now. To my amazement I watched a row of four camels pass along the other side of the road.

'What are they carrying on their backs?'

'Can't you smell it?' Mahin asked.

'Yes, it stinks!'

'Exactly, their own dung – wonderful fertilizer for the gardens in springtime.'

Then a man riding a donkey passed in the opposite direction.

'Unbelievable,' I exclaimed, 'but unlike us, at least these four-legged creatures are actually moving.'

As we inched slowly along, a red Maserati passed in the opposite direction. It looked so incongruous. 'What on earth is that doing here?' I asked.

'Some people have money. It probably belongs to the son of a wealthy bazaar merchant.'

'Or a mullah?' I suggested.

'That's also possible when he's not wearing a turban.' Mahin laughed.

A little further along was a man with a stall selling ladies' underwear. I watched in disbelief as the street vendor held up a bra and demonstrated its chest and cup size – with his fists – to several chador-clad women.

'That's unbelievable.'

'Why?'

'Men selling ladies' underwear in the street. I can't believe what I'm watching.'

Mahin gave me a quizzical glance.

Next to him, a grinning man was holding two live geese upside down by their feet. More eye-catching still were the groups of glamorous young ladies in Western fashions and high heels, their vivid appearance more noticeable amongst the groups of chador-clad women.

'This country is a complete paradox and Tehran the most enigmatic and eclectic city on earth!' I exclaimed.

Mahin shrugged her shoulders again. Then, after what seemed like eternity, the taxi pulled up in front of the bazaar.

'Hang on tightly to me,' Mahin ordered, as she paid off the driver, 'or you may get lost, and if I'm left alone, I'll surely get my backside pinched!'

Passing through an archway, we entered another world. Mahin explained that trade had been carried on hereabouts for thousands of years. Tehran, in spite of having been little more than a village less than a century earlier, had for millennia been an important place for trade on the Old Silk Route between Europe and China. Almost anything and everything could be bought and sold here.

The bazaar covers an area of several square kilometres, and the passageways exceed 10 kilometres in length, making it what Americans would probably call the world's largest mall.

I felt as though I had entered a vibrant rabbit warren. As we wove our way through the throng, I held on to

Mahin tightly. Each time she stopped to ask the way, I took the opportunity to admire the vaulted brickwork and the elaborate and ornate tilework above our heads. The stalls set out between the brick arches almost defied description. There were sacks of nuts in volumes that boggled the imagination and piles of fruits and vegetables, some of which I had never seen before. The bazaar, which was arranged in sections or departments, seemed like a chaotic labyrinth of Aladdin's caves, filled with goods from all over the world. Through it a heaving mass of humanity was struggling to find what they wanted at prices they were willing to pay. Eventually we reached the jewellery bazaar.

Mahin continues:

Obviously, there was something important I wished to show John – just to ensure he hadn't forgotten what he still had to do.

'I thought you might like to see the rings.'

'I understood we came here to buy a carpet.' John appeared a little surprised – and possibly nervous.

'That's right, but let's begin with the jewellery, shall we?'

I watched John as he looked at all the turquoise; there was a veritable sea of turquoise in shop after shop. He was beginning to look overwhelmed, so I took him by the arm and led him into one of the shops. All the jewellery was set out under glass counters, and John marvelled at the array of rings, cufflinks, brooches, bracelets, necklaces, and encrusted jewellery boxes on display.

John continues:

Mahin opened a discussion with a shopkeeper. To my amazement he took out several pairs of gold cufflinks with turquoise studs. Mahin lined them up and asked me to state my preference. Then she started bargaining.

I was puzzled. Why was Mahin buying me gold cufflinks? Was it to try and put me under some kind of moral obligation to buy her a ring? Ten minutes later, following a very heated discussion that I could not possibly follow, she grabbed me by the arm in apparent disgust and almost dragged me out of the shop. The shopkeeper shouted at Mahin, who raised her nose in the air for the umpteenth time. The shopkeeper shouted again. Mahin stood still and shouted back.

'Come on, let's go, John.'

The shopkeeper shouted again. Mahin stopped once more and slowly turned around. Finally, a deal was struck. The cufflinks were wrapped up and placed in my jacket pocket.

'There's one golden rule when bargaining, John. Whenever a shopkeeper asks you how much you want to spend or what your budget is, never, never, never answer that question. Just act as if you didn't understand what he said.'

'And never pay the first price asked?'

'Absolutely not. If you do that, the shopkeeper won't sleep for a week.'

'How's that?' I asked incredulously.

'Why? Because he'll curse himself that he hadn't asked

for more. The merchants never expect to sell anything for the asking price. And another point,' Mahin continued. 'Never go shopping in a hurry – you'll be the loser.'

Mahin then manoeuvred me into another shop selling similar items of jewellery. I watched in utter disbelief as she asked the shopkeeper to place yet more cufflinks of the same design on the counter.

A few moments later she asked me an astonishing question: 'Have you got those cufflinks I bought you?'

'Yes, here you are.' I pulled the small box out of my pocket and placed it in Mahin's hand.

She opened the box and placed the cufflinks on the counter for the shopkeeper to examine. There was another exchange of information, and then the shopkeeper disappeared with the cufflinks to the back of the shop.

'He's Armenian. I trust him more than the shopkeeper next door.'

The Armenian returned and Mahin began haggling with him. Then she took back the cufflinks and began pushing me – by now I was utterly perplexed – out of the shop.

'Whatever next?'

'I thought as much – he's a rogue. The cufflinks we just bought were guaranteed 18 carat gold. The Armenian said they're 16 carats and is willing to swear as much on the Bible.'

Back in the first shop, Mahin placed the cufflinks on the counter and accused the shopkeeper of being 'al dang' – which I knew to mean rogue – and a thief, and demanded her money back. The shopkeeper went white with rage, cursing Mahin and the Armenian and calling them both liars on the Holy Koran. Mahin was as unsurprised as she was unmoved at his reaction. She patiently stood her ground until she got her money back. Then, taking the same cash, she hauled me back into the Armenian shop and bought the 18-carat gold cufflinks for the same price, just as the Armenian had promised.

'John, you seem to be puzzled that I've just bought you some jewellery. How do you call those things in English?'

'Cufflinks.'

'Yes, that's right, cufflinks. Don't you understand why I bought them for you?'

I was puzzled. 'As an expression of love and affection, perhaps?'

Mahin smiled. 'Answer me another question: when the police make an arrest, what do they use to lock up their prisoner?'

'Cufflinks. No sorry, handcuffs!'

'Now you have it. In Iran, when a girl buys her lover cufflinks, it's a sure sign that she intends locking him up. Now let's look at the rings. Are you going to buy me one, John?'

I had never seen so many rings and so much jewellery illuminated under so many bright lights in my entire life. I had often walked down Bond Street in London, but this was really something else.

'Yes, Mahin, I will buy you a ring, but I think it only fair I talk to my family first. Would that be acceptable to you?'

She looked at me quizzically, pursing her lips.

'When, John?'

'As soon as I have returned from England, I will buy you a ring from one of the famous jewellery shops in Zurich. But what I could do – since you have already stolen my heart – is buy you a locket to put my photo in and hang around your neck.'

'Very well then, I will have to wait a little longer for my ring.'

Seconds later, the Armenian, who had evidently been following the English conversation, produced a tray full of gold lockets.

'Here, John, I would like this one.'

I produced my wallet and paid the sum Mahin had negotiated.

'Now let's go and look at the carpets.'

Progress was slow – we turned left and right so many times I wondered how we would ever get out of this enormous bazaar. Yet it was fascinating and, judging by the small number of Europeans mixing in the crowds, something of a tourist trap. Occasionally we emerged into open-air courtyards before being once again enveloped by the bargaining hoards. Finally, we reached the carpet bazaar: a large open space surrounded by numerous shops stuffed full of carpets of all sizes and descriptions. Mahin explained that carpets were bought and sold here by the ton and exported all over the world.

Two men invited us down into a huge cellar. Floodlights were turned on, revealing pile upon pile of carpets.

'Now you know why I brought you here. I guessed we'd be coming down into one of these basements. Just imagine, if I was alone…' Mahin continued a little nervously. 'We're going to look at a lot of carpets now, and when you see one you particularly like, just gently tap my foot, but not in such a way that anyone sees you doing it.'

For half an hour or more two men turned piles of carpets. Eventually, three were selected and pulled out on top of the piles. Mahin began bargaining. The prices went to and fro. To indicate disagreement, Mahin lifted the end of her nose by raising her head. It appeared to me to be a very rude gesture, but it is entirely acceptable in the Tehran bazaar. After another half hour a boy came down the stairs with tea, and discussions briefly stopped.

Mahin looked at me. 'Don't answer this question,' she whispered. 'Which one do you like best?'

I returned Mahin a look of incomprehension, but I gathered that I was supposed to tap her foot when she looked at the one I liked most. The bargaining resumed. As soon as they had finished their tea, Mahin turned to me and said, 'Let's go.'

'Go where?'

'Out, of course.'

'Why?'

'Stop asking questions and climb those stairs!'

I followed Mahin up the stairs out of the basement. One of the dealers persisted in shouting at Mahin, but she ignored him. At the top of the stairs, he jumped in front of her from behind and pleaded with her. Mahin turned up her nose. He mentioned another price. Mahin turned up her nose and offered another price. There was a pause. Then all three of us descended into the cellar again. Some 15 minutes later it appeared to me that a deal might soon happen, but

I was far from sure. Such was the tension that one of the merchants was working his worry-beads at lightning speed while the other chewed ever faster on an unlit cigarette.

I had expressed my preference for a blue and white Kashan carpet about three metres long and two metres wide. It now lay on top of all the others. To my complete astonishment Mahin took off her shoes and crawled all over it on all fours like a Persian cat. Five minutes later she triumphantly declared that she had found a missing thread. The bargaining was reopened, this time for defective goods, which, of course, justified a further reduction in price.

Throughout the negotiations, Mahin remained poker-faced, although she seemed to be enjoying herself. The shopkeepers, on the other hand, appeared to be thoroughly disgruntled. She turned to me. 'They keep asking me to stop bargaining and let that foreigner pay a decent price. When I told them you might one day become my husband, they seemed to believe it, and their morale completely collapsed.'

One of the men addressed me directly.

'She very hard woman.'

'Are you going to cry then?'

They didn't understand. Mahin translated.

'Yes, yes!' they screamed. 'We cry!'

Little did they realise that I was wondering if one day she would make me cry too. What if the ruthless way she dealt with bazaar merchants might, on occasion, be replicated in dealing with her husband?

I looked at my watch and shivered: two hours so far, and still no deal. Finally, Mahin asked them to tie up the

Kashan carpet and call a porter. Very slowly and carefully, in a manner worthy of Shylock, Mahin counted out the banknotes, double-checking them before parting with them. At the top of the stairs, she instructed the porter, who by then was bent double under the load, to stop a moment. Hanging from the wall near the front door were small handmade carpets, and as we walked out of the shop, Mahin put her hand up and helped herself to one of them. One of the shopkeepers shouted at her. Once outside she shouted back – as she translated for me later – that she didn't bring foreigners into the bazaar for her own pleasure and that she was entitled to a commission on the transaction. I was flabbergasted, and as Mahin turned to walk away, I turned and looked over my shoulder a final time and was astonished to observe a tear run down the cheek of one of the shopkeepers.

'Mahin,' I whispered in her ear, 'you're just so ruthless, you've actually reduced one of those men to tears.'

'You're joking!'

'No, I'm absolutely serious.'

She looked back in disbelief and noticed him wiping a tear from his cheek. Then, apparently overcome with compassion, Mahin rushed back into the shop and pressed a 20 tomaan note into his hand.

I was entirely perplexed by her mercurial response. How would I ever understand this woman?

'Where are we going now with this carpet?' I asked.

'We're going to meet Fereydoon and Mahdokht for lunch, and then I hope Fereydoon will put the carpet in his car and take it home for me.'

'But how on earth are we going to find them in this rabbit warren?'

Mahin stopped again to ask the way. The porter struggled on under his load. He seemed to know where he was going, and we followed him. Some 10 minutes later he staggered down some stairs into a basement and put the carpet down just inside the door. Mahin paid him off and he disappeared.

'This is one of the oldest restaurants in Tehran. It's what we call a *Sofrehkhaneh*.' ('*Sofreh*' meaning 'tablecloth' and '*khaneh*' meaning 'house'.)

The restaurant was an extensive, brightly lit saloon, with a pervasive aroma of delicious food. The structure of the building consisted of beautiful brick vaulted ceilings finished in highly elaborate plasterwork and supported by arches spanning between brick columns. A small group of musicians, seated beside a central fountain, accompanied a vocalist who was singing traditional Iranian songs. Around this, there were slightly raised platforms in the ancient form of a traditional *Sofrehkhaneh*. They were bedecked with cushions, like ancient saddlebags, for diners to lean on as they sat, cross-legged, on Persian carpets, whilst old carved wooden benches, tables and chairs were arranged around them. Beyond this, the external walls of the restaurant consisted in part of ornate wooden Persian lattice screens infilling the voids beneath each arch. Between other columns, ancient Persian paintings were displayed depicting exotic damsels, reminiscent of the time and way of life of Omar Khayyam. Looking up I could see a gallery, a mezzanine with more tables, around the centre of the restaurant.

'Traditionally, places like this were patronised principally by men, but there was some space for families upstairs,' Mahin explained.

In a far corner we found Fereydoon and Mahdokht seated at a table.

'We were getting hungry,' Mahdokht explained, already tucking into a salad.

Leading me away to another corner of the restaurant, Mahin was anxious to show me all the Persian dishes. 'Now, John, you must choose,' she insisted.

'The aroma is just amazing, and all of it is healthy, I guess?'

'Exactly so.'

'I'm going to take the national dish, chelo kebab. It was so good last time, and I really don't know when I'm going to taste it again.'

As soon as we were all seated around the table, I held Mahin's hand firmly in mine, and looking across at Fereydoon and Mahdokht, I broke the news that I would be returning to Switzerland in a few days' time.

'Oh no! But surely, you'll come back? How can you forget Mahin?' Mahdokht enquired with pleading eyes.

'I shall never forget Mahin or any of you for as long as I live. I'm so grateful to you all. I've been so lucky. You and all the Iranians I've met have been so kind and hospitable. I've had a truly remarkable stay here in Iran.'

'What about you, Mahin? Don't you want to see John again?'

'Don't worry, Mahdokht, I know for sure that John will come back. He's leaving his heart here with me locked up in this locket he's just given me. And just to make sure, I've bought him some gold cufflinks to tie his hands as well. You see, no other woman will be able to touch him before he comes back.'

Fereydoon looked up from his plate and glanced at me in wry amusement. Evidently, he thought his sister was joking. I was less sure. I had already learned that Mahin invariably had the courage of her convictions. Underestimating her determination was a mug's game. Indignantly she stared at her brother.

'Do you doubt what I'm saying? You know I'm always right.'

'Yes, of course.' He appeared to acquiesce, but as the waiter arrived with our lunch, he asked, 'Who chose the carpet this morning?'

'John did. It's a beautiful blue and white Kashan.'

'Well, sister, at least you'll have that little secret to yourself to remember him by.'

Sometime later the waiter served traditional Iranian desserts and offered us a small glass each of a saffron sherbet.

'Where have you parked your car?' I enquired. 'It must be almost impossible around here.'

Fereydoon smiled. 'Don't worry. I have a friend who's taking care of it.'

I helped Fereydoon carry the carpet up the stairs and out of the restaurant and then hailed another porter. A good hour later he stopped his car outside my residence in Shah Reza Avenue. Embracing Fereydoon to say goodbye, I found myself still having difficulty adjusting to Iranian culture, which proscribed any public display of affection between persons of the opposite sex, whereas men kissing men bordered on the mandatory. I promised to call Mahin at her office on Saturday morning.

Two days later Harry arrived from London with my replacement. The three of us soon sat down to in-depth discussions about the project. Harry opened by explaining his concerns and recalling how the project had been chosen by the empress Farah.

'This project is more like an artist's dream than anything that might eventually get built,' he suggested.

'I share your concerns. Only last week we held a long meeting with a US manufacturer of air conditioning systems. They arrived in the offices with their Iranian representatives, and I had the distinct impression that they were more concerned about their commissions than providing any services. In some ways the extreme design of the leaning towers suggests that this project belongs more in fantasyland than in the real world,' I said.

'Conspiracy theories, eh?' Harry suggested. 'Could it be that some people in the know deliberately presented the design fully expecting that it would never get built but could earn them some fees? Maybe we really are in fantasyland! But never mind. Whether it eventually gets built is not our concern. In the meantime, we need to earn and get paid our fees.'

I was booked for my return trip to Switzerland the following Tuesday. There was no denying that my imminent departure filled me with a profound sense of foreboding. Would I ever return? I had decided to spend my last night with Mahin at Leon's Grill on Shah Reza Avenue. We would dine on caviar and share our last hours together. From there we would go straight to the airport in time for my flight departing at two in the morning.

Later that afternoon, I took my replacement around the offices, introducing him to his future office colleagues and bidding them goodbye. Before finally leaving the office, I knocked on Caroline's door as I knew she was still curious about my beautiful girlfriend. She looked up at me, expectantly.

'Have you brought those photos, John?'

I put my hand in my breast pocket, pulled out two photos and handed them to Caroline. I watched her face change.

'Good heavens, she's utterly amazing, one of the most beautiful women I've ever seen! No wonder you've fallen in love. What man wouldn't? I can't believe you won't come back.'

'Caroline, I really don't know. Just thinking about leaving is painful enough and thinking any further ahead than that is even more excruciating. My brain is completely anaesthetised.'

Caroline handed the photos back. 'You won't find a girl like that in Switzerland. She's in a class apart. I'm betting you won't be able to get her out of your mind.'

On that final evening, we arrived at Leon's Grill and sat at a table under cedar trees in a secluded corner of the garden. An instrumentalist was playing a santoor accompanied by a man tapping on a drum with his hands. The strained magical sound of the santoor resonated around the garden. I had never heard such an extraordinary musical instrument in my life.

Noting my curiosity, Mahin explained, 'The santoor originated several thousand years ago in ancient Persia. As you can see, it's played sitting down with a pair of special mallets. It has 72 strings mounted on a trapezoidal sounding box. The tone of the music varies according to how close to the bridge the player hits the strings. My father plays it quite well, but it takes a lot of practice.'

'What a wonderful sound. It's absolutely magical,' I replied.

A waiter arrived with a bottle of vodka encased in a block of ice, while another waiter placed a huge glass bowl full of ice cubes in water on the table. On top of the mounds of ice he placed two small, shallow bowls filled with black caviar and on the table two little copper cylindrical lamps to warm the blinis. Then he poured vodka into each of the two small shot glasses.

Mahin continues:

John was looking a little lost. I smiled at him. 'Haven't you tasted caviar before?'

'No, never. This is the first time. Please show me what I should do.'

'First you heat a blini by placing it over the flame in the little lamp stand. Then you put it on your plate, like this. And then you take a small amount of the caviar with the special bone spoon and spread it on the blini. Then you can squeeze a little lime juice on it and take it in your fingers and put it in your mouth like this.'

'And the vodka?' John asked.

I picked up my glass of vodka and swallowed its contents in one gulp.

'Like that!' I exclaimed, my eyes almost popping out of their sockets.

John followed.

'Do you often drink vodka?' he asked.

'Frankly, no, but my father – much to my mother's disapproval – drinks it every day when he comes home from work.'

'And why does your mother disapprove?'

I smiled, remembering the many 'discussions' my parents had on this topic.

'She fears that he won't be admitted to paradise with her, and he always replies in the same vein, claiming that in hell there is vodka while in paradise there is surely none.'

When the caviar was finished, we dined on a green salad and ordered the king of all fishes to follow: chargrilled sturgeon kebab marinated in saffron and lemon juice and served with rice.

John, squeezing his lemon on his kebab, declared, 'For as long as I live, I shall never forget the taste of this fish. I really think it should only be consumed in paradise. Although, frankly, given the choice of sturgeon kebab or caviar, I would take the kebab.'

'I'm inclined to agree with you. Are there any sturgeon in those beautiful Swiss lakes?' I asked.

'No, only trout and carp, as far as I know.'

'So, no paradise in Switzerland, John?'

'No, Mahin, I've reached the conclusion that paradise is here with you.'

That was the answer I was looking for, and it led directly to my next question.

'So why are you leaving?'

John continues:

'Frankly I wish I wasn't, but I have to go where I can find work, and there is nothing for me here. You seem quite relaxed that I'm going, Mahin. Won't you miss me?'

'Of course I'll miss you, John.' There was a girlish manner about her tonight. Was she toying with me?

'Then why are you so relaxed? I'm not even convinced you're really in love with me.'

'Not in love with you? You think I would marry a man I don't even love? Are you crazy? We're just very different.'

'That's certainly true. But how do you mean?'

'Because you, John, you wear your heart on your chest. Isn't that what you say?'

'On my sleeve…'

'OK, on your sleeve for everyone to read. But I'm not like that. I keep my emotions inside me – that's the way I am – but it doesn't mean I don't have any. It's just that I don't show them in the same way you do.'

'Really, how can I believe that? You're certainly very passionate, Mahin, and, despite what you say, very extroverted.'

'Being passionate is something else; you've seen nothing

yet. Come back and I'll show you what passion really is. As for my emotions, you'll have to believe what I tell you. That's why I'm so sure you'll come back, since if you don't, there'll be two broken hearts. Your heart has spoken to me, and I know it can't live without me. It's that simple.'

She seemed so sure, and I was so uncertain. We were certainly different. The silence between us was laden with unspoken concerns.

'When will you come back?'

I didn't answer this directly, as I had no idea what to say.

'Mahin, can't you see how difficult such a marriage will be? Not only do we have nothing in common – no shared interests – but our cultural backgrounds are so different. Are you ready to say goodbye to your family and friends and your wonderful job just for me? How do you know that you will be happy living in Europe?'

'John, you must understand, it's as though you fell out of an aeroplane at my feet. A young man with blond hair and blue eyes – you're a dream come true, an opportunity to marry a man of my own choosing! Really, you don't understand. I've never given my heart to anyone, ever. I've given it to you – only you. Please don't break it. I promise I'll follow you wherever you lead me, no matter what I have to suffer.'

I hesitated. Mahin was so sure of herself and spoke sincerely. What would any man say to this smiling *houri* from paradise? What man would have the courage to turn her down, and then manage to put her out of his mind? Her self-confidence was as intoxicating as it was disarming. Contradicting her would be pointless, and truth be told, no matter how difficult or terrifying the possible consequences, I neither wanted nor had the guts to disappoint her.

'Well, I could take some leave in October possibly.'

'Then come back in October, and maybe we can get married. But first you must promise to send me a ring, one with diamonds all around.'

'You mean an eternity ring?'

'John, give me your hand.'

I put one of my hands on the table in front of her. Removing one of her rings, she slipped it on to my little finger.

'There you are – it fits perfectly. Now you know my size. Before you send it, you should have it engraved with your name and the date you proposed to me. All right? You promise?'

'I promise,' I replied hesitantly while trying to stop my hand from shaking.

At 11 o'clock, as the restaurant was closing, we made our way back into the street and hailed a taxi.

By midnight I had checked in, and my departure was imminent. For a short while we sat together in the airport terminal holding hands while she continued sliding her ring on and off my little finger as though to remind me.

Before it was time for our final goodbye, she opened her handbag and pulled out a small sheaf of airmail envelopes with her address typed on them in Farsi script.

'Here you are. These will be delivered faster since they won't need to be translated for the postman first,' she explained. Again, I found myself in awe of her self-confidence and composure.

I opened my briefcase and handed her a bunch of similar envelopes addressed to my office in Zurich. By now I was fighting back tears, and Mahin was wiping them away with a tissue, almost as though she was a nurse caring for a patient. I detested displaying my own weakness, but I was powerless to prevent it. How did Mahin manage to keep so much self-control?

Finally, it was time. Mahin stood in front of me holding my hands in hers, her big black eyes staring at the tears running down my cheeks. She looked so serene. My heart was in my mouth; she could have been torturing me. She was just so perfect, so strong and so very beautiful.

Mahin continues:

John had questioned my composure several times, but it wasn't an act. As I tried to explain to him, I have always successfully managed to keep my true feelings locked up inside me. My passion was no less real for being hidden. Normally I would disparage people who lacked self-control, but in John's case it was different. John appeared to cry easily and quickly and at all times of heightened emotion. But rather than ridicule that, I loved it as part of his wonderfully open heart. I had found a man that was truly honest and not afraid to show his love for me and not afraid to speak of this love. I knew from our initial meeting that my own heart would be safe with John. As I said, I believed I could read him easily, and the way he looked at me enabled me to become even more confident, more composed, because I felt secure. So, although my feelings dwelt deep inside me, I did believe one day I would be able to share them with him.

I was as certain as it was possible to be that he would come back. Even without the strength of our love and our declarations, there was the matter of our destiny. Despite my assertions to the contrary, I felt confident that the fortune teller's prediction was being fulfilled. John would come back. There was no possible way by now that this was coincidence. Something greater than either of us had decided we were to be together; it was preordained.

I had after all stolen his heart already, and I knew – even if he had yet to accept it – that he couldn't live without it or without me.

The terminal was almost empty, but there was an irritating security guard who seemed fascinated by us. He was watching us almost openly, which was highly distracting in our last few moments together. 'John, give me a five-tomaan note please.'

John took out his wallet and handed me a note. I walked over to the guard and, handing him the note, invited him to go buy himself a drink somewhere. Then, returning to our secluded corner in the terminal, I put my arms around my lover and leaned in close to whisper.

'John, you cannot fight a force that is stronger than you are. Stop crying. Go and buy me a ring and come back and marry me in October.'

John drew in a deep breath. Placing one hand around my waist and the other behind my head, he kissed me ardently, and we held each other in an embrace I hoped would never end. Moments later he was gone.

When I arrived home that night, it was a little before dawn. I went straight to bed, and for the first time since my childhood I wept uncontrollably. It was as if everything I had tried so carefully to hide suddenly burst free. The strength of my emotion actually frightened me. Unquestionably, I was in love; I had no doubt about that. With every part of my being, I wanted John to be the embodiment of the fortune teller's prediction. I knew he loved me, but whereas it had been easy to appear confident when he was with me, now I was alone again just as before. Had I been deceiving myself in believing I could just carry on as normal? I claimed to have taken John's heart from him, but in truth I had given him mine also. It was impossible for life to proceed as it once had, as – long before I met him – I had been dreaming about this blond-haired, blue-eyed lover. Now he had actually flown away from me. Just when I thought my tears were exhausted, they seemed to consume me once more. Had I really expected him not to go? To change his mind at the last minute? Did I really believe I had that power…?

I had begun to calm myself somewhat, reassuring myself that if this really was destiny, there was no reason not to expect John to return, when a new and contrasting worry took hold. What if he did come back? What if everything I wished for came true? I would have to honour my promise, of course, but had I truly thought about what that entailed? Could I really face leaving my country and my family and the job that I loved for an unpredictable life in a foreign country? What if I didn't fit into my new home – if I felt out of place or homesick? I found myself consumed by tears once more until eventually I fell into a fitful sleep, a sleep in which the image of the abyss played endlessly in my conflicted mind.

12

THE AGONY AND THE ECSTASY

Your love has made me drunk; my hands are trembling.
I am intoxicated. I don't know what I am doing.

Mevlana Jalaluddin Rumi

John:

As the aircraft gathered speed, the flickering oil lamps marking the runway brought to my mind that – just like Hasan-i-Sabah's Fedayeen – my visit to paradise was over. I was being returned to the world I had left just seven weeks earlier. My real world. Why had Mahin not drugged me with hashish before take-off? Or maybe she had, and I hadn't noticed. Once airborne I pulled a rug over my face and body and tried to put Mahin out of my mind by sleeping. I also wished to hide my bloodshot eyes from those around me.

A few hours later I was awakened by the smell of breakfast. Opening my blind, I could already see the Alps in the distance. We touched down on time, and as

I disembarked at Zurich Airport, I instantly knew that I was back to reality. I took the bus into the city centre and walked to the office, arriving just as the office manager opened the door. We spent a good hour talking about Iran and the 'shah's gift to his people'. I said nothing about Mahin. Maybe it was jet lag, but already my Iranian adventures seemed like a fairy tale.

That evening, I drove out of town and moved into a guest room, above a restaurant, in a village just outside the city. I placed Mahin's photo on my bedside table as a memento from paradise. Now she was thousands of miles away. Was she real or just a dream? My heart ached just looking at her. The photo – lifeless as it surely was – stared straight back at me. What was I going to do?

Mahin continues:

After my tortured night, I had pulled myself together. I determined that the only thing I could do was to put John out of my mind and concentrate on my work and studies. Our destiny notwithstanding, it was now up to John to fulfil his promise. There was very little I could do to affect this at present.

A couple of days following John's departure my phone rang.

'It's Tahira here. I've been talking to Azar.'

'What's she been saying?'

'Not very much.'

'What's that mean?'

'She told me that you've been going out unchaperoned

with that gorgeous European man with blond hair and blue eyes.'

'What else?'

'That I should phone you if I wanted to know more.'

'Well, he flew back to Switzerland a couple of days ago, and that's that. Satisfied?'

'But if he's really in love with you, then surely he'll not just forget you?'

'That's his problem.'

'Not if we're to believe what the fortune teller said. He'll come back. After all, a house has already come into your name, and you've met a man with blond hair and blue eyes. All you need do now is travel the world with him.' Tahira paused.

I didn't really want to talk about this with her, but I found myself correcting her.

'The fortune teller didn't say that I would travel the world in the company of the man with blond hair and blue eyes.'

'Maybe not – but that is what Azar and I understood.' Tahira paused again.

'Well, in that case you understand too much.'

'I swear he'll never forget you. In fact, I'm sure he's left his heart behind in your care. No man who has ever fallen in love with a girl as beautiful as you are will ever get her out of his head. If he hasn't already proposed, I think he soon will, either by phone or letter.'

'That's enough speculation. I must get on. My minister's calling.'

It was an excuse, but it was sufficient to make Tahira

hang up. However, she had succeeded in bringing John once again to the forefront of my thoughts.

John continues:

The following weekend I decided to climb the Rigi, the mountain between Lakes Zug and Luzern known as the 'Swiss Queen of Mountains'. The exercise would clear my head, and I could spend the day trying to reach a decision about my relationship with Mahin. I determined to climb the mountain and return, all within a single day.

The following Sunday morning I parked my car near the small town of Arth at the southern extremity of Lake Zug, put on my walking boots and began trudging up the mountain path.

It was now early summer, and there was a pervasive smell of freshly cut grass that was rather invigorating. On the lower slopes the tinkling of cowbells rang out across the green fields. Further up, sheep were grazing in the clearings between the trees. After plodding uphill for some four hours, I paused and sat down on a wooden bench in the shade to admire the view and take refreshment. Beneath my feet Lake Zug glistened like glass in the sunshine. I was just able to identify the chalet on the edge of the lake where I had spent carefree summer vacations with my family not so many years before.

It was mid-afternoon by the time I sat down for a late lunch at the Rigi Kulm Hotel. I picked up an information leaflet as I came in and checked the height of the Rigi summit: 1,800 metres. I sat down and ordered a light snack, and my mind wandered back to the mountains I had seen. To put this 'Swiss Queen of Mountains' in context, Mount Damavand, just 50 kilometres east of Tehran, is at least three times as high. In other words, this 'Swiss Queen' is a molehill by comparison.

Whilst I ate, I pulled Mahin's photos out of my rucksack and placed them on the table in front of me. What would happen if a sudden breeze blew them away? Would I chase them, or would my problem have simply disappeared in the wind? But there was no wind. Rather, there was a choice, one of which was to take a flying leap off the precipitous edge of the Rigi summit a few yards away, the other to marry her. I couldn't bring myself to make a decision and like a coward promptly put the photos back in my rucksack, settled my bill and began the descent.

About two hours later I stopped and sat down under the shade of some trees to think. I felt very angry with myself. I despised myself for my own fecklessness. I refused to accept that I was a hostage to my own emotions, and I hated myself for it. Mahin was so strong and self-confident she made me feel weak. In contrast to my own conduct, she behaved decisively – fully aware of what she wanted. It's true I cannot hide my emotions. I really wish I could, but that's just the way I am. On the other hand, I believed that even if Mahin concealed her feelings, it didn't mean she didn't have any. She knew exactly what she was doing to me, and – without cruel intention – she obviously enjoyed every moment of it. Was I just a plaything for her amusement? She was always so fearless and so persuasive in her manner. She had the qualities to seduce the strongest of men. Furthermore, she had an extraordinary instinctive ability to see through people almost instantaneously. She was never taken in, and if she had ever been cheated, she must have learned quickly never to be deceived again. She was charismatic as well as assertive, but like so many Iranians, she was utterly infuriating. In other ways she was really like a *houri* – a lethal instrument whose role it is to cut a man's heart out. As she surely had with mine.

I also knew that if I was uncomfortable in my predicament, I had only myself to blame. At the races, Veronica had tried to warn me. I should have grasped that in a non-permissive society, girls are not looking for casual affairs as they often are in the West. Rather they are looking for long-term relationships in the form of marriage, and any man who chooses to promote such a relationship should first consider how it will likely end. That surely was what Veronica had been trying to tell me. Years ago, someone told me that if I wanted a casual relationship, I should choose someone less attractive to ensure I didn't fall in love with them. In Mahin's case that advice, too, had been comprehensively thrown to the wind. I also recalled another friend – a female friend – telling me that there would come a moment in my life when I would see the woman I would marry and that she would burn a hole in my heart – on sight! That surely was what had happened to me.

To be quite frank, I had never imagined that I – or anyone else for that matter – could fall in love so quickly, so dramatically and indeed so inconveniently. I had always imagined that deciding to marry someone would be gradual and incremental, a logical, measured process that would naturally take its course. How wrong I was!

So many questions plagued me. Why was this stunningly beautiful woman still single? Had she been European, she would doubtless have attracted numerous suitors. So why me? And what about that episode in the bazaar and the utterly ruthless way she dealt with the carpet seller? Surely my predicament was even worse – I was the wretched carpet! I was a miserable emperor euphemistically deprived of his clothes.

I pulled the photos out of my rucksack. 'Go on, tear them up!' I urged myself. 'They're just paper. Why let them terrorise your mind?'

I began thinking about the letter I was going to write breaking everything off. But my thoughts were swamped by memories. For a blissful few minutes, I imagined myself back in the garden of the German Hotel dancing with Mahin under the stars. My lips moved as though I was talking to her, in the words of the ghastly, painful letter I was planning to write. But first I must destroy those photos. While contemplating this voluntary act of destruction, my emotions took possession of me, and tears streamed in rivulets down my cheeks, until the mountains in the distance beyond Lake Zug appeared blurred, as if viewed through a car windscreen in torrential rain.

Some minutes later I managed to regain some composure. I looked across the lake, and the mountains were clearer now. I took a deep breath and looked again at Mahin's photos before packing them away. I had capitulated. It was beyond me. My life would never be the same again; I was compromised in love, and I would have to bear the consequences no matter what. Tearing up those photos was simply impossible. I stood up and began wandering slowly down the mountain path. I now knew that if I didn't marry Mahin, I would spend the rest of my days forlornly looking for her. I would never be happy.

The following Monday lunchtime I went to a jewellery shop in Zurich's prestigious Bahnhofstrasse and chose the most expensive white gold eternity ring I could afford that fitted my little finger and – just as Mahin had asked – had inscribed on it 'John, 27 May 1969'. A week later, when it was ready for posting, I brought the ring and Mahin's photos into the office and showed them to my astonished office colleagues. The following weekend I flew to England and announced my extraordinary news to my even more astonished family.

Mahin displaying her engagement ring.

13

CIRCUMCISION

Beyond the earth,
beyond the farthest skies
I try to find Heaven and Hell.
Then I hear a solemn voice that says
'Heaven and hell are inside'.

Omar Khayyam

Mahin:

'This needs a signature, madam.'

Returning home from work one Thursday afternoon, I found a postman standing outside my garden gate. He was holding a small package, and from the way he seemed to be leering at me, I imagine he'd guessed it was of some significance.

I looked at him. 'And a generous tip as well, I suppose?'

'Well, madam, I've been waiting here some considerable time.'

'Really?'

'Yes, ma'am. I decided it might be very valuable and that I should put it safely in your hands myself.'

I duly signed and fumbled in my handbag to find him a tip. Once indoors I put the envelope down on my dressing table and looked for some scissors. Slowly and carefully, I opened it, and sure enough, there inside was a small box containing a white gold eternity ring. Taking a deliberate slow inhalation of breath, I lifted the ring for closer inspection. John had been true to his word; it was inscribed with his name and the date of the proposal.

With an air of gravity, I slipped it onto my finger. It was a little large, as my fingers are very slim, but it was exactly what I had asked for.

It was now time to face the reality of the situation. Hitherto my love affair with John had been something wonderful, but I had not been entirely honest with myself; I wanted his love, but I had been reluctant to contemplate the potentially life-changing consequences. Yes, I had enjoyed his company and undeniably found him very attractive, and yes, I had admitted both to myself and to John that I was in love with him. Nevertheless, somehow it had suited me to live from day to day in a state of denial – to avoid the painful process of making difficult decisions: giving up my wonderful job, leaving my family and friends, walking away from my new house (which I still had to furnish properly) and starting life all over again in a strange country.

Sitting at my dressing table I wondered whether I had been just too carried away by the romance of our meeting. It had all the hallmarks of a wonderful fairy tale: a handsome blond hero, a mysterious prediction, a whirlwind love affair made all the more intense by our inevitable separation. Would it possibly have been more perfect to leave it there? A love that had too many obstacles to be ever consummated unattainable and therefore unspoiled by reality.

And what a reality it would be. If a wedding was to be arranged, it would fall to me to deal with all the complications, the negotiations and the inevitable bribes. John wouldn't have any idea of the difficulties involved. Why should he? I stared at my reflection in the mirror. What had I been thinking of when I had said *yes*?

I looked again at the ring. It was just what I had asked for. Convincing myself that I just needed a little more time to think, I slipped it from my finger and put it back in its box.

But I had promised… I picked up John's letter to reread it. He mentioned a date in October when he proposed returning to Iran to marry me. It was less than three months away. I could not delay my decision much longer. Either I must make my news known or return the ring.

The following morning John rang from Switzerland. He sounded excited. His voice always reassured me.

'Has it arrived?' he began.

'The ring, you mean?'

'Yes, has it arrived?'

'Yes, John, it's arrived safely.'

'Does it fit? Are you wearing it?'

'Yes, it fits, but I'm not wearing it yet. I'm waiting for a suitable opportunity to see my father and announce our engagement to my family.'

'Please call me after you have spoken to your parents.'

'It'll have to be later in the week. I'll call you again in a few days.'

John sounded a little disappointed. Maybe I didn't sound suitably excited.

Later the same morning Azar rang to ask if John had sent me a ring yet. It was clear that I couldn't escape the subject.

'Yes, Azar, he has. It arrived yesterday, but please, not a word to anyone until I've told my family.'

'There you are. Didn't I tell you? It was obvious that he couldn't forget you. When's he coming back?'

'In October, according to his letter.'

'Wow! Just a few months away. Have you thought about all the consequences?'

'Such as?'

'Such as whether or not he's been circumcised. Have you asked him, or maybe you've checked for yourself?'

'What an impertinence! The questions you ask! No, I haven't checked; nor have I asked him.'

'Maybe you should ask him…'

'But he'd be terrified if I asked him such a question. I don't want to frighten him away.'

'You know as well as I do that there's no way around it. If he's not already been done, then he'll need an operation. Then you'll really find out how much he loves you, won't you?'

I couldn't believe I hadn't thought about this. Yet another complication I would have to address. John would undoubtedly be horrified…

'Honestly, Azar, that's enough. I'm going to hang up!'

A few days later I decided the time had come to visit my parents. I had lost too much time already in reflection and had come to the conclusion that our marriage was inevitable. If the fortune teller was to be believed, then it was actually my destiny, and I should stop questioning it.

Nevertheless, I was a little anxious about explaining it to my parents, so I wasted no more time and told them immediately on arrival.

They stared at me in utter astonishment.

I carried on enthusiastically. I told them all about John and how he had proposed to me. I explained about his job and his life in Switzerland and what little I knew about his parents.

'But you've just bought a house. Surely you don't intend to accept his offer, Mahin? And what about finishing your education?' my father enquired. 'Seriously, are you in love with him?'

'Father, I fell in love with him almost the moment I first saw him. Now that he has left, he keeps writing me letters, and every time I read them, I weep. His words are so charged with emotion. I cannot possibly disappoint him.'

I opened my handbag and took out John's ring. 'Father, if you agree, then I will put this ring on my finger now.'

My mother gestured to me to let her see it. 'This isn't an Iranian ring,' she exclaimed.

'No, Mother, it's Swiss.'

'But you said he was an Englishman.'

'Yes, as I explained, he lives in Switzerland. It's all rather complicated.' I opened my handbag again and produced

John's photograph and handed it to my mother. I watched her reaction as she looked at my handsome suitor.

'He has blond hair and blue eyes!'

'Yes, he does. He has an administrative job in the construction industry. He was here in Tehran for several weeks working on the new headquarters building for the National Iranian Oil Company, and now he's gone back to Switzerland. He plans to return to Iran with his parents in about three months' time to ask for my hand in marriage and, if you agree, marry me. Then we'll go and begin our lives together in Switzerland.'

My mother was aghast. 'What – you mean leave Iran and go and live in Europe?'

'Are you sure about this, Mahin?'

And I was. Despite all my earlier doubts and concerns, as I heard myself justify our love to my parents, I knew without question that I was making the right decision.

'Yes, I'm quite sure. I've known it from the moment I met him. I understood almost immediately that he would make a wonderful husband and a wonderful son-in-law for you too. He's a dear man. He's utterly devoted to me. He's so pure, so honest. I know in my heart that he will take care of me for the rest of my days.'

I looked at my father. 'You will agree, won't you, Father? When he was here initially, I was a little in denial of my love for him, and I didn't know if I should take him that seriously. Besides, it all seemed too complicated. But now that he's gone, I realise that I really want to share my life with him.'

'My dear Mahin, you know very well that I'll not stand

in your way. But I really do hope that this is a sensible decision.'

My mother disappeared into her bedroom.

'I'm sure of it, Father. I'm quite certain that he absolutely adores me. His heart is in mine, and as I already explained, I cannot possibly disappoint him now.'

My mother reappeared from her room carrying a small box, which she handed to me. It contained a white platinum ring set with a huge diamond surrounded by small white gold leaves on which were mounted several smaller diamonds.

'Put your engagement ring on your finger and then put that one on top to make sure it stays in place. I've been keeping it for you for this very day.'

I did exactly as my mother had suggested. Then I stood up and embraced her.

'Mother, that's absolutely wonderful! I must go and have some photographs taken and send them to John.'

Once I had answered all my parents' questions, I made my way home. Before I left, I had to agree to my mother's suggestion that she should organise a family party for the following Friday. A celebration of my engagement. It was actually all coming to fruition. I was officially engaged.

To begin making arrangements, I called up a professional photographer to attend the family reunion and take photos that I could mail to John. Then I wrote a letter to John to tell him how well our news had been received and about the celebration, during which I would be photographed wearing my engagement ring.

The following day Tahira rang.

'I've just spoken with Azar. She told me the news. Congratulations, Mahin, that's wonderful. You see, I knew it would happen as predicted. It's all coming true! Have you told John about the fortune teller's predictions?'

'Tahira, I don't understand you. If you really believe all those predictions, you should be more worried than ever. Have you forgotten what you were told? As for telling John, no, I haven't told him anything. If he knew that, there's no knowing how he might react. Or perhaps that's what you want me to do, to break this cycle of predictions coming true?'

'I suppose you're right, Mahin, and really, I'm very happy for you. I try not to think too much about my prediction, although there's nothing I can do to avoid whatever fate has in store for me.'

John continues:

When the promised photographs arrived, I think I fell even more deeply in love with Mahin. They were truly stunning and showed off her beauty to maximum effect. She was more beautiful than any movie star I had ever seen. I bought a silver frame and placed it beside my bed. Each night, I looked at her face as I drifted off to sleep and dreamt of the paradise that awaited me.

The following weekend I wrote to Mahin, enquiring about the marriage ceremony and suggesting some ideas for a honeymoon. Telephone calls were more difficult. Sometimes I would go very early to the office and call her from there, but with calls being via the operator, since neither of us had a telephone where we lived, communication was a challenge. Occasionally Mahin called me from her office telephone, but as I was usually in meetings, they were less than satisfactory experiences.

The weeks of waiting dragged into months. Mahin's letters were usually quite light-hearted; in one of them she explained that the postman had found out about her lover in Switzerland and insisted on handing any letter with Swiss stamps on it to her personally. Of course, a tip was expected for this service. But a later letter she sent contained a suggestion that I was not altogether happy with. She suggested that we should not rush into marriage, but rather she should have time to complete her university education. In other words wait another year! I wrote back saying that I didn't think I could survive living alone three thousand miles apart for such a long time and suggested that she could continue her education in Europe. I confirmed that I would return to Iran in the first week of October and that my parents would follow about 10 days later.

On arrival at Mehrabad Airport I passed through immigration and customs without difficulty. I couldn't wait to see my fiancée's beautiful face and I scoured the crowds to locate her. I was disappointed when there was no sign of her anywhere. Just as my heart began to sink, I came across Fereydoon, who greeted me warmly.

'Where is Mahin?'

'She had to go to work this morning. She apologises for not coming to meet you and asked me to come instead.'

I was stunned. 'Is the minister of agriculture more important than I am?'

Fereydoon returned me a wry smile and, taking hold of one of my bags, led me out to his waiting car and then drove me to my hotel.

'You've come back to marry my sister?' he asked rather awkwardly.

'That's my intention. Do you think your sister will agree?' I added, not knowing what else to say. Fereydoon smiled again but gave no reply. This was starting to feel a little stranger than I had anticipated.

'When will she be home?'

'Early afternoon normally. We can go to her house now and wait for her to come back.'

The following three hours dragged. I think I had been so excited to see her again that the extra delay disappointed me. We spent the time at her house drinking tea and making conversation with Mahin's cousin and her husband who both lived downstairs.

After a short while it occurred to me that I had not seen Fereydoon's girlfriend.

'Where is Mahdokht?'

Fereydoon appeared to flinch slightly, and his face took on a melancholy expression. He sighed deeply before answering, 'Mahdokht is no longer part of my life.'

He was silent for a moment as he gathered his strength to continue.

'Her father found out about us. He also found out that Mahdokht's mother was complicit in what he considered our illicit relationship. He was so angry he very nearly murdered his wife. He beat her up so badly that she was covered in bruises. Mahdokht fared little better, and of course, I've not been able to see her since.'

'I am so very sorry.'

'I was utterly heartbroken. For several weeks I shut myself away in my room and spoke to no one. I was becoming suicidal, I think, so finally one of my sisters took control. She found me a wife, and I married her just like that.'

I was astonished at what I was hearing.

'I really can't believe that. You and Mahdokht were both so very much in love.'

'Yes, John, we were, but in the Zoroastrian faith anyone who marries someone who is not a member of their religion is considered to be lost and is excommunicated from the family. Mahdokht's father would never allow that to happen to one of his children.'

'You mean you married another girl with your eyes closed?'

'Yes, John. When I make love to her, I put out the light and try to imagine she is Mahdokht. But of course, it doesn't really work.'

'Don't you love your wife then?'

'Not really, no. I can never love anyone except Mahdokht.'

'But that's horrible!' I exclaimed.

'What can I do? That's the reality of living in this society – we have these terrible religious splits that are quite intolerant of one another.'

After this sad disclosure, we seemed to lose the desire for conversation. We sat in a solemn silence until finally

Mahin appeared. I leapt to my feet as months of repressed emotion coursed through my body at the sight of my beautiful fiancée.

'You came back?' she asked rather sheepishly.

I moved to embrace her, but she held me back, denying me anything more than a peck on the cheek in front of the neighbours.

'How long are you staying?'

I felt a little disorientated. This was not the reunion I was expecting.

'Three weeks... as I told you.'

'I don't think we can possibly marry in such a short time. Anyway, it being Thursday, it's the weekend, and we'll have to see what can be done when work starts on Saturday. In the meantime, I'll take you to see my father later this afternoon.'

Mahin looked at Fereydoon. 'Go and look for that new wife of yours and bring her here later, and we can go together to our parents' house.'

Fereydoon agreed and took his leave. Mahin took me by the arm and led me into her house for the first time. We climbed the stairs to the first floor. Beside the staircase was a lightwell filled with climbing plants surmounted at roof level by a lantern light. As we mounted the stairs, we were serenaded by the songs of canaries flitting from branch to branch in the lightwell. At last, after such a long time we were finally alone. Following such a long separation we had almost become strangers to one another. Our first hours together were uneasy. It took a while until we felt sufficiently reacquainted and we readjusted to one another's presence.

'Are you hungry?'

'Yes, Mahin, I am. Shall we go out?'

'No, I'll cook some ham and eggs if that's all right with you.'

'That'll be just fine,' I replied. 'Have you made any preparations for our wedding?'

'What preparations? I've had no time, and besides, you've not yet met my father.'

'Do you suppose that he'll disagree then?'

'No, I don't think that, but you can hardly expect me to make wedding preparations until he's accepted you as his future son-in-law. Besides, as I said already, I don't think it's possible for me to marry a foreigner in just three weeks. We'll find out on Saturday when the new week begins. Where are you staying?'

'I've booked into the Hilton. What else could I do?'

Later that day Fereydoon returned with his new wife, Parvin. She was dressed in a short white dress, cinched at the waist with a belt. She was not unattractive, but I sensed a coldness between them. It was also apparent that Mahin had not become close to her in the same way she had been with Mahdokht. It was just such an incredibly sad development.

We all got into Fereydoon's car and drove to their parents' residence, a large apartment that still served as a family home. Somewhat anxiously, I followed Mahin up the stairs to the first floor and into a large saloon where her parents were waiting.

As we entered, Mr Rashvand rose to his feet to greet me. Mahin formally presented me to her parents and, after saying a few words to her father, invited me to open the conversation. Breathing deeply, I launched into my rehearsed speech.

'Mr Rashvand, I came to Iran less than six months ago for just a few weeks, and soon after my arrival I had the good fortune to meet your daughter, Mahin. I must admit that I instantly fell profoundly in love with her. In the short time I have known her she has taught me much about the rich history and culture of Persia. I very quickly gained the impression that she is a very wise and mature young woman. I had no plans to get married to anyone, and nor, I think, did she, but nevertheless, after just a few days, quite unexpectedly I asked her, and to my great surprise she accepted. I have found Mahin to be a truly remarkable and very talented young lady. I can only imagine that she is very dear to you and that the prospect of parting with her must surely be a very painful one. Indeed, it is surely a proposition to which you would only agree in the interests of your daughter's own happiness. As for my credentials, I think that Mahin will already have explained, and I do hope that you will have found her explanations satisfactory.'

I stopped for a moment and took another breath.

'I have come here today to formally ask for your daughter's hand in marriage.'

'Mahin has explained all these things to me,' Mr Rashvand replied. 'She has also explained that your parents are coming to visit us. They will be very welcome. Of course, you are right, it is very painful for a father to part with his daughter, especially one as dear to me as

Mahin is. However, she has convinced me that while like you she had no plans to marry, she fully intends to keep the promise she made you. I am therefore pleased to tell you that your offer is entirely acceptable to me, and I have much pleasure in welcoming you into our family as my son.'

I promptly stood up, put my hand in my pocket and took out the small box containing Mahin's engagement ring. Mahin rose to her feet and held out her left hand for me to put the ring on her third finger. Mr Rashvand embraced me and kissed me on both cheeks while his wife stood up and, to my utter astonishment, took my head in her hands and kissed me on the lips.

Her husband then walked across the room and opened the door of a large cabinet and took out some glasses and a bottle of vodka and placed them on a tray. He filled two glasses, and passing one to me, he linked his right arm in mine, and together we drank the vodka in one single gulp. As we returned to our seat, Mrs Rashvand began to serve us fruit and nuts taken from a huge bronze bowl on the carved wooden table.

'Mr Rashvand, in England we say that in the interests of a successful marriage it is a husband's role to make his wife happy. Do you say the same thing in Iran?'

A broad smile spread across Mr Rashvand's face.

'Yes, we do, of course we do. But, John, you should have asked me that question first not last! Let me warn you now that making an Iranian wife happy, except perhaps for a few moments at a time, is all but impossible. They always complain. Worse than that – when things go wrong, they never take responsibility for it. They systematically take the credit for what goes right and blame their husbands for all that goes wrong or whenever their husbands fail to satisfy them.'

I listened to him with amusement, unaware that in the years to come I would often have cause to reflect on that warning.

'Mahin, how should I address your father and mother?'

'You should call my father *Agha Joon*, which loosely translated means "dear sir", and my mother *Hanjoon*, which is short for *Hanoum Joon*, meaning "dear madam".'

'But I heard your mother address your father by your family name, Rashvand. Is that usual?'

'In our culture, at least among the older generation, wives will usually address their husbands in that way. We are very formal. Like the Germans, we love titles. My father calls my mother *Hanoum*, meaning "madam".'

'Do they do that all the time?'

'As far as we are concerned, yes. How they address one another in private is their affair.'

A little while later, Mrs Rashvand invited her guests through to the dining room. On the table was a veritable pile of saffron rice. The main dish was *koresht-esfenadj*, or spinach stew.

At that, *Agha Joon* raised his glass and proposed a toast to the bride and groom. The rice dish was followed by baklava. Just as I assumed that the meal was finished, more family relations arrived – and progressively more and more – until the evening moved on from a dinner party to a large family reception. Unsurprisingly, Mahin was determined that I should meet not just her parents but as many other members of her family as possible, all of whom were enthusiastic to meet the 'new Englishman'. It was almost midnight when Fereydoon dropped me off at the Hilton.

Mahin continues:

The celebration had gone very smoothly. I admit to feeling rather proud to show off my fiancé, and I noted that many of my relations were equally fascinated by his striking colouring. I realised then that most of my doubts were behind me. There were still, however, many bureaucratic obstacles to face, obstacles that John could not possibly have envisaged. The most challenging of these was the requirement for me to obtain permission from SAVAK, the Iranian Secret Police and Security and Intelligence Service, to marry a foreigner, a procedure likely to take anything between three and six months. John would also need to apply for a residence permit, and then there was the difficult question of his circumcision. It was a subject I had not yet mentioned to John, but it would be a requirement. Yet John had expressed his astonishment that I had made no preparations for our wedding. If only he knew!

The following day, my hand was trembling as I picked up the phone and called General Zahedi to see if he could help me. Until recently he had been my boss as Minister of Agriculture and had recently been promoted to Minister of the Interior. He invited me to call and see him at his ministry the next morning.

John continues:

On Saturday morning I walked to Mahin's house, and from there we took a taxi. Some 15 minutes later we pulled up in front of an imposing office building. Without saying a word, Mahin led me into a lift. Emerging on one of the upper floors, we entered a large vestibule, and she gestured to me to sit down on one of the vacant chairs while she spoke to the receptionist. After exchanging a few words, she promptly disappeared through another door.

Fifteen minutes went by, then 30, and still nothing happened. The lift doors opened, and four men appeared, one following the other, carrying three huge baskets of flowers between them. Each basket was about the size of a small bathtub. I looked on in silent amazement. What is this place? I wondered. Where are those flowers going? A bribe, perhaps, or an expression of gratitude?

A few minutes later Mahin reappeared. 'Follow me.'

I followed her along a corridor. She knocked on a door, and I followed her in. An official sitting behind his desk stood up to greet us. He pointed to two chairs and went to close the door. The official talked to Mahin for some 10 minutes, then turned to me and, in impeccable English, said, 'I understand it is your wish to marry Miss Rashvand. Wonderful!'

'Yes,' I replied. 'That is indeed what I hope to do.'

'Hmm,' said the official. 'I'm afraid it's rather complicated.'

'How's that?'

'I don't think you know where you are, do you?'

'No, not really. All I know is that I'm in Tehran, but I don't know where in Tehran I am.'

'Let me explain. You are in the offices of the Ministry of the Interior. Miss Rashvand has just had an audience with the minister, and he has passed me some verbal instructions.'

'I see.'

'Let me begin by explaining that any Iranian national wishing to marry a foreigner is obliged to obtain written authorisation from our national security organisation, which we call SAVAK. How long are you staying in Iran?'

'Three weeks.'

'Well, I'm afraid it takes a minimum of three months to obtain this permission.' I stared at him, somewhat vacantly, trying to digest the information.

'The minister has asked me to find a solution to this time constraint.' He picked up his telephone and following a brief conversation hung up. He looked at me and smiled. 'Now we have to wait for the answer.'

He then turned to Mahin. 'Has your fiancé obtained a sworn affidavit from the British Consulate in Tehran confirming that he is a bachelor?'

'No,' Mahin replied.

The official turned to me. 'In Miss Rashvand's interest I think you should obtain one.'

A while later the phone rang again. The official picked up the receiver, and a very heated discussion followed. Mahin was smiling, evidently understanding everything. Then he hung up.

'Well, there we are. I've spoken with the SAVAK

officials and asked them to confirm or otherwise whether they have a file on Miss Rashvand. I explained that I was acting on behalf of my minister and that the matter was extremely urgent, pertaining to a matter of national security. I further added that the minister had instructed me to advise them that they must provide the correct answer within 20 minutes, or their jobs would be on the line. So now we have the answer: they have searched everywhere, but despite my insistence that there must be a file somewhere and that their jobs really are on the line, they've been unable to find any trace of one. You can imagine their reaction when I instructed them to deliver a clearance certificate to that effect to my office here within 24 hours, and when they asked why it was required in these extreme circumstances, I explained that Miss Rashvand needs the certificate so that she can marry a foreigner. They're now very angry because they realise that they've been... how do you say?'

'Deceived, duped.'

'Yes, that's it, duped.'

'That's amazing,' I exclaimed. 'You Iranians are truly extraordinary people. We're both so grateful to you.'

Turning to Mahin, the official continued. 'Miss Rashvand, please come back again tomorrow morning for your clearance certificate.'

A few minutes later we were back down at street level hailing a taxi to take us to the offices of the British Consulate. On arrival there was a short queue, but by one o'clock we were sitting in front of the consul himself. I produced my British passport. The consul looked at us both quizzically. 'Getting married then?' he asked, raising an eyebrow.

'Yes, sir.'

'You're the second candidates this morning. It seems these Iranian girls have quite an appetite for eligible young Englishmen. Are you going to swear an affidavit on the Bible or on the Koran, Mr Goodall?'

'I think the Bible will do nicely, thank you.'

I filled in the relevant forms. The consul produced a Bible. I swore and paid his fee. Once outside the embassy compound, we hailed yet another taxi.

'I'm going back to my office,' Mahin declared, 'and you can go home and relax until I come back and cook some lunch.'

'You've told your boss, I presume?'

'Told him what?' Mahin looked at me incredulously. 'That I'm going to marry an Englishman and leave him?'

'Yes, for example.'

'No, I've told him nothing. Why should I?'

I was aghast! We seemed to be living parallel lives. Every reasonable assumption I made, Mahin promptly blew to pieces. I just could not, for the life of me, read her mind.

The next morning, we set off, once again, in a taxi.

'Where are we going today?'

'You'll have to wait and see.' This was Mahin's habitually vague and unhelpful response.

'But first we shall need a supply of passport photos.'

From the photo studio near the Hilton we took a taxi to the Ministry of the Interior to collect the promised papers. An hour later we were standing in a queue in yet another government office.

'What are we doing here?' I enquired.

'Obtaining notarised copies of my birth certificate.'

To me it looked like the height of inefficient bureaucracy – a long queue that hardly moved. 'We'll be here all day at this rate.'

A large photo of his imperial majesty, the *shah-an-shah Aryamehr*, hanging from one of the otherwise bare walls, cast a watchful eye over the queue. A boy was wandering around offering cups of tea for a few rials each. Mahin paid for two cups and simultaneously placed a brown paper envelope on his tray. Ten minutes later the boy returned to collect the empty glasses and gestured to Mahin to pick up the brown envelope.

'Let's go!'

'But we haven't got to the front of the queue yet.'

'What for? There are two prices for the tea. Anyone paying the higher price has no need to wait.'

'You mean you bribed the tea boy? I don't believe this; that's corruption!'

Mahin returned me a look of incomprehension. 'Corruption? What are you on about? Everyone's free to do as he or she pleases. Where's the corruption in that? It's a free country. If those people prefer to wait all day in a crazy queue rather than pay the supplement, that's their choice. It's rather like first- and second-class travel in an aeroplane.'

I was aghast. I looked at Mahin in disbelief, not knowing how to respond. A moment later I realised that several people in the queue were staring at me. They were probably wondering what all the fuss was about. Speechless, I shrugged my shoulders.

'Have you got your passport with you?'

'Yes, why?' I asked, somewhat surprised.

'We shall need a sworn translation into Farsi.'

We walked a little further along the street. On the other side of the road, all along the pavement in the open air, there was an extraordinary sight: a row of men seated at individual desks with typewriters on them. It was as though the entire street had been transformed into an open-air office.

'What on earth are they doing there?'

'They are scribes. Why are you so surprised? A large percentage of the population is illiterate. These scribes type letters and other documents for those people who want to communicate with friends or family in another city.'

I was even more astonished.

'And what happens if the recipient is illiterate as well?'

'Dumb question, John. He goes and finds another scribe, who reads it for him.'

Mahin led me into a small office just off the street.

'Where's your passport?'

I produced it, and Mahin handed it to a man behind the counter, whereupon she immediately began haggling with him. Then he handed her a receipt, and she turned to leave.

'What, you're going to leave my precious British passport in this place?' I remonstrated.

'Yes, why not? I've a receipt for it.' Mahin paused. 'Unless you want to spend the night here.'

I groaned in resignation.

'We'll collect it tomorrow and then we'll need to get you a residence permit.'

'Whatever for?'

'Simple, you won't be eligible to marry me without one.'

'How long do you think I'm staying in Iran?' I added indignantly.

'At least until we're married,' Mahin said. 'Now we can go and look for some lunch.' Further along the street we walked into a chelo kebab restaurant, where we sat upstairs in the family section and ordered some *doogh* to quench our thirst. The restaurant was anything but sophisticated, but the food was good.

'Where are we going after lunch?' I asked.

'I'm going back to my office, and you can go back to your hotel. At about seven this evening, after I've finished work, we'll have supper somewhere.'

That evening we took a meal in the Hilton Brasserie.

'When are you going to hand in your notice?' I asked, feigning nonchalance.

'That question again! I would be mad to do such a thing.'

'Why? If you're coming to live with me in Switzerland, you'll have to leave one day soon.'

'John, I don't think you understand this country. Do you want me to come to Switzerland with you or not?'

'What's that got to do with it?'

'Everything!' Mahin exclaimed. 'And if my minister disagrees?'

'Disagrees? Is he permitted to disagree? What is this country, a prison?'

'Not exactly, but there are limits.'

'Limits? What limits?'

'Well, for example, no married woman can leave Iran without her husband's written permission.'

'You mean, if I don't sign for you, I could just abandon you here, married and locked up?'

'Actually, no, you can't. The law has just been amended such that the rule doesn't apply to Iranian spouses of foreign husbands.'

'And what about foreign spouses of Iranian husbands?' I asked, thinking of Caroline.

'There's no such thing.'

'How do you mean, no such thing. I know at least one such lady.'

'Foreign women, in contrast to foreign men like you, are obliged to take Iranian nationality before marrying an Iranian man.'

'And are then obliged to get their husband's written permission to leave the country?'

'Quite so.'

'But that's not just sexual discrimination – it could also be a prison sentence!'

'Quite so.'

'On the other hand, if a minister decides that he wants to keep his secretary, he might very well decide to keep her. So, what are you going to do then – just walk out, disappear, or what?'

'No, I shall just get on a plane and go when I'm ready, that's all.'

'Incredible!' I exclaimed.

The next day we set off again to collect the sworn translation of my passport and from there to yet another government office to obtain my residence permit. By the time we were sitting in the back of yet another taxi, I had resigned myself to the seemingly unending paperchase, and I no longer bothered to ask where we were going next. This question invariably elicited vague and unhelpful responses from Mahin. Suddenly, the taxi pulled up in front of what looked like a small hospital. Mahin paid the driver and we stepped out. Taking my arm, she guided me through the front door, to reception and from there into a waiting lift.

'Mahin, this looks like a hospital. Where will you take me next? Do you suppose I might be sick?'

'I hope not, but we both have to undergo medical examinations and obtain certificates before we can marry. That includes a blood test to ensure that we haven't got any nasty transmittable diseases.'

'What, chastity clearance?' I asked.

'What do you mean?'

'Clearance to become lovers…'

'Well of course. We don't want any unpleasant surprises, do we?'

'Unbelievable,' I added in utter amazement.

'Why? I actually think it's rather a good idea.'

'Are we going to undergo fertility tests as well?'

'Of course.'

'How do they check that?' I was beginning to feel a little anxious.

Mahin ignored my question as she went up to another

reception desk and came away with a clutch of papers in her hand, which we then filled in before she handed them back to the receptionist together with another sum of money that she asked me to produce. Following a brief wait a male nurse came and invited me to follow him. I looked enquiringly at Mahin.

'Men and women are examined separately. Off you go, and I'll see you back here in a little while.'

Having extracted a blood sample, the nurse took me for an interview with a doctor who asked me to take off my shirt and lie down while he went over my chest. He then checked my reflexes with a rubber mallet.

'Now you can put your shirt back on, stand up and take your trousers down.' I did as the doctor asked and stood in front of him in my underwear.

'And your underpants,' the doctor said firmly. Somewhat surprised, I did as the doctor had asked. The doctor pulled up a stool and fastened his eyes firmly on my pelvic region, carefully placing his hand against my right and left leg in turn, each side of my scrotum.

'That's all right. You can get dressed now. Your certificate will be ready for collection in two hours.'

About 15 minutes later Mahin reappeared and suggested we go off for some lunch and come back later. On our return the receptionist handed Mahin two separate envelopes, which she immediately opened. Having read them she instructed me to sit down while she disappeared once again.

Mahin continues:

It was exactly as I had feared. My fiancé required circumcision. I asked to see the doctor who had signed the certificate.

'This certificate is not what I asked for.'

'You asked for certificates required prior to a marriage. That's what I've given you.'

'Yes, but here you have written that my future husband has not been circumcised. That cannot be correct.'

'But it is correct. I have examined him myself.'

'But in that case, we can't get married.'

'That's not my problem. If you want him circumcised, I can give you a price.'

'How much?'

'Three hundred tomaans (approx $40).'

'Don't you realise that if I tell him that he needs to be circumcised, he'll probably run away?'

'Not my problem. But maybe if he loves you enough, he will agree? I can fix it in just 30 minutes.'

'But he'll be sore for at least a week.'

'Then wait another week before you get married. Or better still, let him run away, and you can marry an Iranian. Then you won't have these problems.'

'Look, all I am asking for is a certificate confirming that my fiancé has been circumcised. Is that really too much to ask?' I insisted. 'Please doctor, I'm really just asking you a little favour, just between you and me.'

'3,000 tomaans ($430),' the doctor replied.

'3,000 tomaans? Are you crazy? That's ridiculous!

Look, I'll lend you my sunglasses and then you can examine him again, and perhaps you will look a little less carefully this time?'

'Madam, don't you realise that you are asking me to commit a crime? It's 3,000 tomaans no less!'

'What, just for a second look? I'm not willing to pay more than 1,000 tomaans'

I began walking towards the door. 'Two thousand five hundred tomaans, last price!' the doctor shouted.

'Out of the question. One thousand five hundred; not a tomaan more.'

The doctor closed his office door in disgust behind me.

'What's up now then? Something wrong with me?' John asked anxiously as I reappeared in reception.

'Nothing wrong with you, just with these people. Never mind, let's go.' A few minutes later we were standing outside hailing another taxi.

'Where are we going now, for heaven's sake?'

'John, you ask too many questions. Please just do as I say and let me ask the questions, OK?'

John continues:

The mystery tour of Tehran continued as we stumbled out in front of yet another office building. Mahin led me inside, up some steps, through some double doors and into a large room. Sitting at the far end was a mullah in his brown aba and white turban with two scribes, one on each side of him. They were sitting at desks with very large books open in front of them. We sat down for a while in the chairs reserved for visitors, and as soon as the seat in front of the mullah became vacant, Mahin got up, sat in front of him and engaged him in conversation. After a little while she beckoned me to come and sit beside her in front of one of the scribes. She had produced various papers, which the mullah had been examining. After a while one of the scribes began writing in his book. I dared not utter a word since I knew that Mahin would explain nothing. Then after about another 15 minutes she turned to me.

'Please give me two thousand tomaans.'

'Two thousand tomaans! That's almost three hundred dollars. Whatever for? Do you know how much that is? It's the cost of a honeymoon for at least a week in the Presidential Suite of the Hilton Hotel. I'll be cleaned out!' I didn't move.

'John, please give it to me.'

'Whatever for?'

'Never mind what for. If you want to marry me, there's no other way but to pay.'

'I don't believe this!'

'You have to believe it.'

Very slowly and very reluctantly I produced my wallet and nervously counted out the money; I handed it to Mahin, who counted it out again. The mullah held out his hand and counted it for a third time. Then the scribe began writing again. After another 30 minutes or so the mullah handed Mahin back the papers she had given him together with something else that looked to me like yet another certificate.

Mahin stood up. 'Let's go.'

I followed her out of the double doors, down the steps and into the street.

'For heaven's sake, Mahin, this is beyond a joke.'

'Joke,' she cried out, 'but it's really the greatest joke!'

Then quite suddenly, like quicksilver, the serious expression on Mahin's mercurial face changed. She was consumed by raucous laughter.

'I'm glad you find it funny. I find it decidedly painful,' I declared.

'Painful,' Mahin shrieked. 'Painful?' She could barely talk. I just stood there staring at the spectacle of my fiancée bent double in front of me. Ever so slowly she managed to straighten herself up, whilst sniggering like a schoolgirl.

'What is all this?' Was something wrong with me? What could be so amusing?'

'Well, I didn't know how to ask you.'

'Ask me what?'

'Ask you if...' Mahin giggled, as tears mingled with black mascara trailed streaks down her face. I waited, stern faced, until she recovered her composure.

'Well, you see, John, had I asked you the question outright, you might have become suspicious, and I feared you might have changed your mind.'

'Changed my mind? About what?'

'About marrying me. You might have taken fright.'

'Mahin, what are you on about? Frightened of what?'

'Of the knife!'

'What, the Assassin's blade, you mean?'

'No, not the Assassin's blade, silly. The surgeon's knife! John, you have just become a Muslim, and your name is now John William Mohammad Goodall.' Mahin broke down again in laughter.

'You mean you've changed my religion without even asking me first?'

'No, of course not. Your religion is what you believe. I can't change that with a piece of paper and two thousand tomaans. You're missing the point, John. A Muslim can only marry a Muslim.'

'But you, Mahin, are not a Muslim, you say!'

'That's right, I don't believe a word of it, but it doesn't mean I'm not one. So, you have to become one as well.'

'But what's all this got to do with knives? You mean I have to be circumcised?'

'Well, my concern was that if I asked you if you'd been circumcised, you would probably have said no and would have then got suspicious. So, when the doctor told me that you weren't, I had to decide what to do. So first I tried to bribe the doctor. He did look at your... didn't he?'

'So that was what he was staring at! And that was what you were arguing about with him down the end of that corridor earlier today. Now I understand.'

'That's right. I tried to bribe him to amend your health certificate, but he wanted a lot of money.'

'So, you bribed the mullah instead, is that it?'

'Exactly, mullahs cost less than surgeons. They always take money. The doctor, on the other hand, was offering a surgical intervention or an even larger sum of money than the mullah to alter the certificate. Would you have preferred that?'

'My God, I'd be sore for a week! But on reflection maybe the real thing would have been less painful than having my bank account circumcised!'

14

MARRIAGE IRANIAN STYLE

Today is the time of my youth
I drink wine because it is my solace;
Do not blame me, although it is bitter it is pleasant,
It is bitter because it is my life

Omar Khayyam

John:

The next day, Mahin explained that we should go and seek out another mullah for the marriage ceremony but that before setting off she would call one of her cousins, who had a mullah in her family. To make the call we went into the local corner shop at the end of the street, which sold groceries and household items. Corner shops in those days had telephones that clients could use in exchange for a few rials. Then we hailed a taxi.

The taxi pulled up in front of a nondescript building in a narrow street. Entering through a glazed metal doorway, we climbed three flights of stairs to knock on an office door. We waited several minutes listening to the shuffling of feet and the closing of office drawers behind the glazed screen. Finally, someone opened the door, and sitting behind a desk was a man wearing a bow tie. His appearance was far too elaborate for a mullah: he didn't have a beard and wasn't even wearing a turban. He invited us to sit down. Mahin began to speak with him for a few minutes before suddenly standing up, grasping me by the arm and pulling me towards the door.

Back down in the street I asked Mahin what that had all been about.

'He's a fraud! Didn't you smell the whisky and see the cigarette stubs in his ashtray? I think he'd only just managed to hide the bottle in his desk drawer before we came in. Did you see that gap between his front teeth? I'll bet he sticks his cigarettes in it, and heaven knows what else besides.'

'He didn't look like a mullah at all to me. Are you sure he was qualified?'

'My guess is that like many other people in this city he has two jobs – for instance a mullah by day and a band leader by night.'

'But what about his beard? Don't all mullahs have beards?'

'Yes, certainly, including stick-on ones. He's just not serious!'

I followed Mahin into another nearby corner shop, and again at one end of the counter was a telephone.

'I've just spoken to my father at his office.'

'Does your father have contacts among the clergy, Mahin?'

'No, not really, but he's just explained that we don't need a mullah. The notary public will do.'

'I thought we were going to a mosque?'

'Not likely. Whatever for?'

Mahin hailed another taxi, and some minutes later we found ourselves entering the office of a notary public. We sat down in front of his desk, and a long discussion ensued, after which Mahin explained that the notary would be coming to her father's house on Thursday evening to perform the marriage ceremony. That was just two days away!

'Mahin, I've been asking you for ages which day we're going to be married. A few days ago, you said it was possibly six months away, and now it's the day after tomorrow. My parents won't arrive for another week!'

'Never mind. Iranian weddings consist of two parts, the *aghd*, which is the legal part, and the *mehmooni*, which is the reception. We'll hold a reception for friends and relatives a week later. They don't need to be present for the legal part.'

I shook my head in disbelief. So many things in this country appeared so utterly infuriating, and in my perception at least, Mahin's unconventional behaviour only served to make matters worse. All events of any consequence always seemed to include a generous measure of the unpredictable.

'Who will be attending the wedding then?'

'My parents and those of my brothers and sisters who are able to come and of course the notary – that's all. Why do we need anyone else? Are you going to buy me a wedding dress, John?'

'What, for the day after tomorrow?'

'No, let's arrange the wedding dress for the reception, and after the wedding ceremony on Thursday evening we can go – just the two of us – to the Hilton for a champagne dinner.'

The following Thursday evening we duly assembled in my future parents-in-law's apartment. Mahin's three sisters were present, together with their respective husbands, one of whom was a general in the Imperial Iranian Air Force and another a colonel in the police force. Her elder brother, Masoud, also attended, with his girlfriend. The notary arrived a few minutes after everyone else. Fereydoon moved the chairs from the dining room and arranged them in a semicircle in the sitting room while his mother passed around cups of tea. The notary sat in the middle of the semicircle with an occasional table in front of him, where he began sipping his tea from a glass cup. He then invited the bride and groom to sit either side of him. Mahin produced a sheaf of papers, which he studied carefully before the proceedings began.

Although I didn't understand a word, I could tell by the tone of the conversation that this family-friendly discussion with the notary was fast developing into a dispute. Then Mahin spoke to Fereydoon, who acted as my interpreter.

'The notary is insisting that you produce a bank guarantee for 750 thousand Iranian rials.'

I gasped. 'Whatever for?'

'Liquidated damages for the benefit of the bride should you choose to divorce her.'

'Seven hundred and fifty thousand rials! That's a small fortune. The sterling equivalent of about six thousand pounds. That's the price of a decent-sized English house.'

I looked at Mahin, who returned my gaze with an unfathomable expression.

'How can anyone ever afford to get married in this country? Why didn't you tell me about this sooner? I would have stayed in Switzerland.' I stood up and looked down at Mahin. 'I can't do this.'

Panic-stricken, she jumped to her feet and grabbed my arm, imploring me to sit down again.

'But what's the point, Mahin? I can't do this. It's hopeless.'

'John, please, I beg you, sit down!'

I shrugged my shoulders and slowly sat down again. Here we go again, I thought, as I recalled a well-worn Iranian expression '*What at first may appear impossible, may in fact be possible.*' Mahin engaged in what appeared to be a furious discussion with the notary, which widened to become a family debate that lasted around 15 minutes. I began to wonder whether I could amend my airline ticket and head back to Europe earlier than planned and put the whole saga behind me.

Then quite suddenly Mahin turned to me. 'I've persuaded the notary to drop this requirement subject to the proviso that you promise to pay me the money at some future date, in which case we can proceed. You just have to pay the notary his fees before he begins.'

Sighing in disbelief, I pulled my well-worn wallet from my trouser pocket and handed the necessary banknotes to

Mahin, who carefully counted them out and handed them to the notary. He wrote some lines in his book, and having recited a few verses of the Koran, he passed the registry book to Mahin for signature and then to me. The signatures were then witnessed by family members. Finally, the notary handed a small green book to each of us.

I flicked the pages and, seeing that it was all in Farsi script, enquired, 'What's this all about? Small print terms and conditions of contract handed out after signature? Highly irregular.'

Fereydoon came to my aid. 'Well actually, no. At least not exactly.'

I returned Fereydoon a suspicious look. 'What then?'

'The books contain advice on how the bride and groom should conduct themselves to enjoy a successful union.'

'I will translate it for you, John. Don't worry,' Mahin promised.

'So, I promise to pay my bride a huge sum of money at some future date, and she promises to translate the clauses of the contract I have just signed at her convenience. Promises, promises...'

'That's it, John. What my sister really means is that she will translate those texts in the book that refer exclusively to what you are supposed to do for her benefit,' Fereydoon added with a mischievous grin on his face.

'Don't listen to him,' Mahin retorted.

'May I kiss my bride now?' I asked.

'Not while the notary's still here, you can't,' Fereydoon replied.

Whether he understood English or not, the notary had

already realised that he was in danger of outstaying his welcome. He began excusing himself and headed towards the door. Fereydoon escorted him out, and no sooner had the door closed than Mahin's father began arranging glasses and a bottle of vodka on the small table where the notary had been sitting. Having filled the glasses, he picked up two of them and, handing one to me, linked arms and knocked the hard liquor straight back in one gulp. I did likewise.

My glass was quickly refilled, and Mahin's brothers-in-law came over to shake my hand and also share a drink. As they congratulated me, Mustapha, the air force general, whispered in my ear, 'Not long ago this family had four pretty daughters, and now they're all married, but you, John, got the best of the bunch.'

Our first kiss in front of family witnesses

Mahin's sisters sat across the room engrossed in conversation, but I could tell by her smile that Mahin had clearly overheard what had been said. I then kissed my bride, which was followed by a round of applause.

Mahin continues:

Our marriage formalities were complete! My handsome blond-haired boyfriend was now my husband. I was quite exhausted with all the running around and the complex organisation, but it was worth it. When he kissed me in front of my family, I felt completely happy. The feeling of security that I had craved settled on me with a tangible warmth. I looked deeply into those clear blue eyes and read the love contained within them. I was his wife, and whether this was chance or destiny, I would look forward to our new life together.

We were to dine alone at the Hilton – a champagne dinner for two – and Fereydoon kindly agreed to act as our chauffeur. On arrival we installed ourselves in a quiet corner of the hotel restaurant. John ordered a bottle of champagne, and for a while we were content to just sit looking at one another as we sipped our drinks and dined on caviar.

Sitting at a nearby table were three young Iranian men who were watching us with much interest. I overheard their conversation, and I translated for John.

'They are asking one another what is wrong with them that their own pretty girls go out with foreigners but not with them.'

'I think you explained the answer to that once before,' John replied.

'Yes, I did, but they're wondering if it's because of your complexion.'

'Are they wrong then?'

To emphasise the point, I turned around and looked even more deliberately and admiringly at my husband.

'Of course not.'

An hour later the champagne and caviar were almost finished, and neither of us wanted to prolong our dining. As far as nourishment was concerned, we were sated. Under the table, our fingers locked tightly, and I felt a rather delicious sensation of nerves and anticipation about what was to follow.

'John,' I said, 'please take me home. I don't want to wait any longer. I've waited all my life for tonight. Let's go.'

John called for the bill. Earlier that day, John had given me some banknotes, so I retrieved one from my handbag and handed it to the waiter. Suddenly there was a babble of voices from the three young men at the adjacent table. 'And what's more, she pays the bill – that's incredible!'

At the front entrance of the hotel the footman hailed a taxi, and some 15 minutes later we passed through the gate of my house. As we walked through the door and up the stairs, I thought of all the nights that I had had to leave John and return to my room alone. All the dreaming I had done here at the end of each date. All the tears I shed when he had left and all the anguish and indecision these walls had been party to. Now I would share my room, and my life, with this wonderful man. What an unbelievable love story this had been – and in truth, it was only the beginning.

And later, as I slipped into the arms of my new husband, I whispered close to his ear, 'I want a boy with blond hair and blue eyes, and we shall name him Cyrus.'

John continues:

The wedding reception was to be on the following weekend, and the ensuing days were taken up in preparation. My parents arrived midweek and were quite stunned by their Iranian daughter-in-law, who addressed them endearingly as Mummy and Daddy as if they were her own parents. Respect for one's elders, it turned out, is a fundamental part of Iranian family values. The day after they arrived Mahin took her new mother-in-law into town to help with the final fitting of her wedding dress. My mother could not help but be amazed at Mahin's tiny waist and slender arms.

In addition to her extensive family, Mahin had invited Betty, her American tutor, whom I had met at the races, together with her Iranian husband. She had also invited several of her college friends and was eager to introduce me to them. Two of them, Azar and Tahira, had brought their husbands, and they immediately bombarded me with questions. A grand buffet dinner was followed by dancing that lasted into the small hours. I took an opportunity to talk with my parents, who were amazed how Iranian society kept up with all

John's father and mother (extreme left and right) with Mahin's father (centre).

the latest Western fashions, from ladies' outfits to dance music.

In the days that followed, Mahin took me and her new parents-in-law to see her relatives in Ghazvin. When the time came for me to fly back to Switzerland, Mahin's passport application and Swiss visa were still being processed. But there were no tears at the airport this time. I was confident that Mahin would soon join me.

Mahin and John (centre). Standing next to John is Azar (after her motor accident) and her husband. Standing next to Mahin is Tahira and her husband (who was to die of leukaemia only months later).

Mahin continues:

Three weeks later I was ready to fly. On entering the airport terminal, I was shocked to come face to face with the deputy minister of agriculture. For a moment I faltered. I had already been missing from the office without reason since the wedding. What would he say?

'Miss Rashvand,' he began, 'we've been missing you. Now I see you're travelling. Where are you going?'

The best way over this hurdle was to tell the truth. 'A few weeks ago, I married an Englishman here in Tehran, and now I'm flying to Switzerland to join him there.'

For a moment the deputy minister appeared stunned. He stood gazing at me wordlessly, while I just kept smiling.

I knew very well that he was a kind-hearted man, and sure enough he quickly began to soften.

'You mean you're leaving us – leaving Iran, Miss Rashvand?'

'Yes, I am.'

'We shall miss you terribly. You really have been the heart and soul of our ministry for such a long time. But what can I say? I've no moral right to stand in your way, or between you and your new husband.'

With a swift glance around, to check we were not overlooked, he stepped forward and embraced me, kissing me on both cheeks.

'I wish you well. Lots of luck and happiness. And, oh, tell that Englishman, whoever he is, that he's a very lucky man!'

Sometime after take-off one of the stewardesses approached me and explained that the captain had invited me to join him in the cockpit. At first, I was taken aback and politely declined, but the hostess was very persistent. Apparently, it was an honour to receive such an invitation. Clearly, she was not going to take no for an answer, and so I relented, although I confess to feeling a little suspicious. The captain and co-pilot got to their feet as I entered the cockpit and invited me to sit down in the co-pilot's seat while the captain explained all about the aircraft. I think I must have been there for nearly half an hour before the plane hit turbulence, the captain handed over the controls to his co-pilot and he escorted me back to my seat before handing me his visiting card and inviting me to call him at his hotel. So that was it. I might have guessed, so many opportunistic men!

When the plane landed, I spotted my husband at the front of the crowd in the arrivals hall. He rushed towards me eagerly and threw his arms round me, gathering me into a huge embrace. He had clearly missed me! As we stood looking at one another and smiling, the flight crew walked past us. In an instant, the captain stopped and looked straight at us. He took a deep breath before continuing on his way.

'What did he want?'

'The captain gave me his number. He hopes I'm going to call him for a night out somewhere.'

'Good heavens! Even before you've landed, it starts. Come on, I'm going to take you home.'

15

REVELATION, DEATH AND REVOLUTION

Poor soul, you will never know anything
of real importance. You will not uncover
even one of life's secrets. Although all religions
promise paradise, take care to create your own
paradise here and now on earth

Omar Khayyam

Zurich December 1969
John:

We had only been married a few weeks and were so passionately in love that most mornings we felt more exhausted than the previous evening. This was especially true at weekends when I did not have to rush off to work. One Saturday morning over breakfast as we sat staring longingly into one another's eyes over fresh croissants and coffee, I heard the sound of a letter dropping through the mailbox of our apartment. I went to pick it up, and seeing that it was postmarked 'Iran', I handed it to Mahin.

She tore the envelope open and began to read while I sat intently watching, amazed that I was now in fact married to my *houri* from paradise. As I watched, an expression of alarm flashed across her face. Then she winced and clenched her fist before thumping it repeatedly on the table, screaming in Farsi words I could not possibly understand. Then finally, staccato fashion in English, 'I don't believe it! I can't believe it! It can't be true!'

Alarmed and bewildered, I got up and placed my arm around her shoulders to comfort her.

'Don't believe what?'

Mahin hesitated. Several seconds passed before she answered my question.

'You remember my friend Tahira and her engineer husband who came to our wedding reception?'

'Yes, of course, what's happened?'

'He's got leukaemia and has less than six months to live.'

'That's terrible.'

'Yes,' Mahin went on, 'but that's not all.'

She paused again as she caught her breath, but she was so distressed that several minutes passed before she was able to compose herself sufficiently to begin talking.

'John – I never thought I would tell you this. I hoped I wouldn't need to... You remember my other friend, Azar, who also came to our wedding with her husband?'

'Yes,' I replied. 'I do.'

'Do you remember she had some scars on her face and neck?'

'Yes.' I thought for a moment. 'But they weren't very obvious, why?'

Then, drawing a deep breath, in an anguished voice, Mahin declared, 'John, I've struggled with this ever since you asked me to marry you, but I've never found the courage to tell you. But now I have no choice…'

I turned my chair around to sit opposite Mahin as I held her in my gaze.

'I'm all ears.'

Mahin continues:

And I told him everything. I told him about the fortune teller and the reputation this woman already had for accuracy. I told him of my initial reluctance to go and about the place she lived in and even the coffee grounds. I tried to be as clear as possible, but all my words came out in a rush, and I kept being overwhelmed by my emotions. I could see John looking at me with some kind of mixture of horror and sympathy, but in all honesty, I could no longer spare his feelings.

He kept his arm around me, and I leaned into its comfort as I told him of the terrifying fortunes of my two friends and how both of those fortunes had now been realised.

As he continued to look at me in amazement, I knew only too well what his next question would be.

'What about your fortune, Mahin? What were you told?

I had no choice but to continue. I owed him the truth.

'The fortune teller had no hesitation in telling my fortune. She confidently revealed three things. Firstly, something would come into my name. Secondly, I would meet a man with blond hair and blue eyes. And thirdly, I would travel the world.'

I looked up at John. An expression of incredulity spread across his face. 'You're not serious?' he asked. 'I don't believe it!'

'John,' I continued, 'every word of what I've told you, on the Koran, on the Bible or any book you like, I swear I'm telling you the truth. You see, just a few months later my father gave me the money to buy a house, and then, when I saw you at the races that day, I knew immediately what would happen. Don't you remember, after Betty managed to introduce us and you told me you were visiting Iran for just a few weeks, how reticent I was to meet you? Had you been permanently working in Iran, we could have married and lived together in my house while I continued to work at the Ministry of Agriculture and completed my university studies. What I feared most was that if I fell in love with you, you would take me away from my family, my job and my studies. But then I remembered the fortune teller saying that I was to travel the world, and now that is exactly what has happened.'

'And all your friends at the races that day... they all knew the story of the fortune teller?' John asked.

'Oh yes, absolutely! That's why we were all looking at you. They were all saying, "Look, there he is!" Believe me, I was shivering in fear – and anticipation.'

'Why didn't you tell me before?'

'I was afraid that if I told you, you might take fright and break off our relationship, so I decided against it. Besides, I didn't really want to believe the fortune teller's predictions. I was in denial. Until today I wasn't convinced it was that important. But with this terrible news from Tahira that her young husband will soon die, all the fortune teller's predictions will have come true: Azar's car accident, and then quite unexpectedly I bought a house and then met you, a man with blond hair and blue eyes. It's absolutely terrifying. I can no longer deny or hide the truth.'

'So that's it, I've been framed!'

'*Framed*, John? *Framed?* What do you mean?'

'I mean that it was a put-up job – all arranged in advance.'

'Yes, John, but be fair. Would it not be more reasonable to say that *we* were *framed*?'

I looked at him anxiously, hoping none of this would affect his love for me.

'Do you regret marrying me now?'

'No, Mahin, I don't regret marrying you. How could I? You're the most beautiful creature I've ever had the good fortune to set eyes upon, and what's more, you're also a quite extraordinary person in so many ways. I'm sure you'll always be a wonderful wife, but heaven knows it's been stressful.'

We sat in silence as the time passed, but I felt my strength and sense of security return as he embraced me. I didn't regret sharing what I had previously kept hidden, as it was in fact our own history.

John continues:

A few days later I called in at the immigration offices in Zurich to progress my application for Mahin's permanent visa and was told that this would be refused unless she held British nationality like her husband. This was a major setback. I had taken out a long-term lease on an apartment, and now all my plans to continue working in Switzerland appeared to be in jeopardy.

I had enrolled Mahin to study German at the local Goethe Institute, which she was quite enjoying. In the evenings after work she would explain to me the similarities between Farsi and German grammar, and she began making such rapid progress that even with my own knowledge of German, I could not answer all her questions. Most of the other students enrolled with her were Czech refugees who had fled their country following the uprising against the Soviet occupation the previous year. For Mahin, this was a totally new and stimulating environment. She began telling me stories of how all the male students would surround her during the morning break, competing for her attention. There was a student sitting just in front of her who was constantly turning around to look at her rather than paying attention to the teacher. When the break came, this young man presented her with her own portrait! Sometime afterwards, she declared that her teacher had almost certainly fallen in love with her and was offering her private lessons free of charge after hours.

At this, I drew a very deep breath and finally decided that we had no choice but to return permanently to England.

Mahin wearing her wedding dress in England when we held a Church Blessing in January 1970

It wasn't easy. Virtually all my savings had evaporated on setting up house in Switzerland, not to mention getting suddenly and unexpectedly married in Iran. When, in January, Mahin announced that she was expecting our first child, my elation was tempered by extreme stress. Fortunately, my employers in London offered me a job, which was excellent news. Unfortunately, though, the job did not come with a Swiss salary. Initially we were obliged to live with my parents in a house that was far too small for two families, and several months passed before I was able to rent another house in the neighbourhood.

I was curious to see how Mahin adjusted to her new European environment. Most people we met assumed that she was either Spanish, Italian or possibly Greek. Only very rarely did anyone surmise that her origins might be somewhere much further east. Most baffled of all must have been the shopkeepers and staff of some of the Oxford Street department stores in London.

Mahin had brought her bartering skills back with her to England; the English were ill-equipped to deal with this form of trading. She would spend the day apparently window shopping and would not express an interest in purchasing any item until 10 minutes before closing time, whereupon rather than pay up and leave she would begin bargaining, fully aware that the staff had buses and trains to catch. Once the doors were closed, she would persist in offering half price and refusing to leave unless it was accepted. Threats to call the police to have her removed were studiously ignored while she insisted on the general manager being called. She would then work her charms on him. Half an hour after closing time, he would have had enough and more often than not would eventually capitulate. As an Englishman, I found her brazen behaviour highly embarrassing. Yet it became commonplace. I invariably tried to keep my distance, but Mahin was undeterred and almost invariably got her way. I witnessed shopkeepers giving in to her persistent bargaining simply to be left in peace and then saw them shout 'No! No! No!' when she started over again on yet another item of merchandise.

If she was rude to shopkeepers, the flip side was that she could be charm itself when she had something to sell. In retrospect, I should perhaps have invested in having her English perfected, and she would surely have thrived in a commercial environment, such was her ability to melt the hearts of men.

Occasionally she would be stopped in the street by a photographer. That was an experience that would never have happened to her in Iran, and she undoubtedly found it flattering. I mused that perhaps she could have modelled jewellery, but as a young man I was far too jealous of my beautiful Iranian wife to seriously contemplate such an idea.

In any event, poor Mahin suffered from morning sickness for the entire nine months of her confinement, and when finally, our first son, Cyrus, was born, she weighed less than before she became pregnant. For all our joy, surviving on one meagre salary in England was really hard. To be fair, Mahin did find part-time employment in the Linguistics Department of Reading University, but her earnings contributed little to our living expenses.

With a small child to care for and little time to study, I began looking at the possibility of finding an assignment abroad, if possible, in Iran. In the spring of 1972, I found an opportunity with the National Iranian Oil Company in Abadan. Following the nationalisation of the Anglo-Iranian Oil Company in 1953, most of the British expatriates had left, but some posts could not easily be filled by Iranians, who in some instances lacked the necessary skills. There was evidently no shortage of Iranian architects and engineers, but the quantity surveying profession as practised in the UK, and as a system still practised in the offices of NIOC, did not exist elsewhere in Iran.

Initially, on arrival, we were accommodated in a hotel, and after a few weeks we were assigned a company bungalow. The summer heat in Abadan is legendary, sometimes reaching 50 degrees Celsius with very high humidity. It rarely rained, but on the few occasions in the winter months when it did, the entire region was inundated. Hardly had we settled down when Mahin announced she was expecting our second child. In April 1973, Darius was born in a nearby hospital in Khorramshahr.

Now back in Iran we had an opportunity to meet old

friends, including both Mahin's friends, Tahira and Azar, individually. I was still wondering whether the whole story about the fortune teller was really true. After all, it is a big ask to believe such stories; anyone could make them up. Tahira, now widowed, confirmed the story in detail, as did Azar, who didn't hesitate to show me her scars. I therefore reached the conclusion, given the complete coherence of all the explanations, that the story of the fortune teller really was authentic.

The following month we were on the move again, this time to work on the Lar Dam and Mazandaran Irrigation Project on a remote site about 30 kilometres east of Tehran. We were allocated a very attractive three-bedroom bungalow in a small village in a deep river valley downstream of the Latiyan Dam. This dam complimented the Amir Kabir Dam near Karaj to the west of Tehran in supplying water to Tehran. The proposed Lar Dam would feed still more water from the Lar River high in the Alborz Mountains via a tunnel into the reservoir behind the Latiyan Dam. This was the first time I had worked on civil engineering projects – initially access roads and tunnels – and the experience gained was to prove very useful at a later stage in my career.

In the wake of the Arab-Israeli Yom Kippur War in 1973, the Gulf Arab states temporarily halted oil production while the shah cashed in and began selling as much oil as Iran could produce at triple the previous price. As a consequence, the Western economies fell into deep recession, and it was just a matter of time before the shah began spending his windfall. Businessmen flocked to Tehran. Some of them, for lack of available rooms, contented themselves by sleeping on the floor of the reception area in the Hilton Hotel before setting off around the city the next day knocking on almost any door that might yield a lucrative contract. Overnight it seemed, Tehran had become the world's honeypot. The Iranian currency was floated on the exchanges and became one of the most sought-after currencies in the world. Many European countries dropped all visa requirements for Iranian tourists seeking vacations abroad. Oxford Street in London's West End was soon filled with Iranian shoppers.

As Tehran house prices soared to ludicrous levels, an inevitable construction boom ensued. At its peak, simple labourers rested on their laurels in the main squares, their shovels upturned and plastered with notices advertising their non-negotiable daily prices at different rates for working in the sun or the shade.

Soon enough I came into contact with my previous employers in London, who, in common with so many construction consultancies, expressed an interest in opening an office in Tehran, and this followed in 1975. In retrospect, supporting that initiative was probably the worst decision of my career.

On the back of the house price boom, Mahin sold her house and bought a larger one. By 1977, a year after we had moved in, it was worth more than a similar sized house in London's Kensington. Of course, in retrospect we should have sold and got out, but rising house prices are invariably intoxicating. They soon become the 'new normal'. Eventually, however, the Arabs began selling their oil again, and as oil prices began to tumble, the market in Tehran progressively turned negative. A pervasive feeling of malaise settled over the country, and a sense of uncertainty became palpable. Then in the autumn of 1977, an American living just a few doors away in the same street where we lived was assassinated. That should have been sufficient warning of the horrors that were to follow.

Mahin continues:

In the wake of the oil boom, in 1971, John secured a job in Iran, and finally in 1975 we were able to return and live in my house in Tehran together with our two young sons, Cyrus and Darius.

It felt strange to be back in Tehran, but I had become accustomed to moving around, and I found myself to be sufficiently adaptable. I believed I was fortunate in my husband and in the two young sons I had wished for. In comparison to many of the marriages that surrounded me, we had found love and a loyalty that underpinned all that fate had in store for us. So, when people enquired if I was happy, I would not hesitate to concur that my marriage was all I had hoped it would be.

In the spring of 1978, Margaret Thatcher, who had recently been elected leader of Britain's Conservative Party, visited Iran. The reasoning behind the visit was that Iran had become the UK's most lucrative export market and in anticipation that she would become Prime Minister at the upcoming general election, she should visit Iran to further promote the commercial ties between the two countries. John had become an active member of the Irano-British Chamber of Commerce, and whilst attending a reception we were introduced to Mrs Thatcher. Immediately curious of how we had become husband and wife, I briefly explained to her how we had met.

In retrospect, I regret that I did not take that opportunity to familiarise Mrs Thatcher with my prediction of the eventual collapse of the Soviet Union and the threat of militant Islam. Whether or not she would have believed me might not have mattered, but when she subsequently saw these hugely important events unfold before her eyes, she might well have been less surprised.

Desmond Harney (Morgan Grenfell, Merchant Bank) introducing Mrs Thatcher to guests in the garden of the British Embassy in Tehran (spring 1978).

A huge garden party hosted by the Industrialist Mohammad Irvani,
Founder of Melli Shoe, at his country residence near Karaj, to which
he invited most of the diplomatic corps and members of the various
Chambers of Commerce represented in Tehran. Mahin is sitting between
her parents-in-law with sons Darius and Cyrus in the foreground
holding party ballons (autumn 1978).

In the autumn of 1978, there were serious disturbances
in the streets as the shah's regime began to disintegrate.
By December that year, like so many of my compatriots,
I became very concerned that major political change was
almost inevitable. Fearing the worst, I was possessed
by the need to do something myself to prevent it. On
Christmas Day we drove through numerous disturbances,
including dodging around barricades of burning tyres in
the streets of Tehran, to visit my long-standing friend,
General Hussein Jahanbani.

A soldier conducted us through the military complex to the general's quarters, where we found him seated behind a desk in his expansive office. Three other army generals were present, one of whom was visibly bleeding from a wound to his forehead recently sustained while directing troops in the streets.

'So, this is the young Englishman you recently married, Miss Rashvand? It's a real pleasure to meet him,' the general exclaimed, offering me and John seats in front of his office desk. 'What brings you to see me today?'

'Well, firstly, my husband and I have come here to thank you for what you have done for us.'

'Done for you? What have I done for you?'

I recounted the story of the fortune teller and how we had met at the races thanks to the general's complimentary invitations.

'That's a wonderful story. I'm very happy for you both.' Turning to John, he added, 'You picked up one of our very best girls. I'm really very envious.'

John smiled.

'Is that the only reason you came?' the general added.

I opened a bag I was carrying and placed a large brown envelope on his desk.

'What's this?' he cried, somewhat alarmed.

'That,' I replied, 'is the future of our country. Open it.'

General Jahanbani looked nervously at the envelope and, pushing his chair back, placed his hands on its arms, distancing himself from what he quickly assumed was something sinister. 'What is it?' Very slowly and reluctantly he leaned forward and tore open the envelope to reveal a neatly folded black chador. 'That's horrible! Why are you doing this to me?'

'Because you're a general in the shah's army. What are you going to do to save our country?'

'Me, why me? What can I do? I am a servant of His Majesty. I'm not in politics. I follow his orders. What else do you expect me to do? If the regime changes, then I'll follow the instructions of whichever government is in power.' A moment later there was a crackle of gunfire outside the window. 'You see – we're trying to suppress this uprising.'

'But you, General, swore a personal oath of allegiance to His Majesty, and now you nonchalantly declare that you will swear another to Ayatollah Khomeini. Are you mad? Do you really suppose that the next regime will trust you? Most likely they'll kill you. Can't you understand that?' I asked.

'It won't happen!'

'It will if you don't do something dramatic to prevent it,' I warned.

'Miss Rashvand is right. If it goes on like this, the regime will certainly fall,' one of the other generals chipped in.

'And you'll all be dead,' I added.

I looked at all these men standing around, mutely accepting of their inability to change anything, and I felt a great rage growing within me.

I screamed at Jahanbani. 'If the shah's regime falls, the entire Middle East will be unhinged! Can't you grasp that? There will be anarchy everywhere. The entire world economy will be shaken to its foundations. Why don't you understand?'

General Jahanbani's face turned as white as a sheet. For a moment he was speechless.

'What are you going to do about it?' I insisted.

Outside the window we could hear shouts of '*Allah Akbar!*' and '*Magbar Amrika!*'

General Jahanbani searched in vain for an inspiration from the blank looks on the faces of his fellow officers before putting his head in his hands while staring at the black chador on his desk.

It was then that I realised I was wasting my time. If these generals could not understand what was about to happen, what could I do? Exasperated, I got to my feet.

'General, you're our only hope. You must stop this revolution. If you don't, you're all dead!'

General Jahanbani didn't move. He didn't even say goodbye.

'Come on, John,' I said. 'It's finished here. There's no hope. The fortune teller was right. Let's go pack our bags and travel the world.'

16

AFTERMATH

Human beings are members of a whole,
In creation of one essence and soul.
If one member is afflicted with pain,
Other members uneasy will remain.
If you've no sympathy for human pain,
The name of human you cannot retain!

Sa'adi Poem placed at the Entrance
of the United Nations Building NYC

John:

In January 1979, in the light of the fast-deteriorating political situation, the British ambassador, Sir Anthony Parsons, had appointed me one of a small number of designated wardens in the area of north Tehran where we lived. I was to be responsible for coordinating the safety of British expatriates living nearby. Early in January 1979, I, together with the other wardens, was called to attend a meeting at the British Embassy chaired by Sir

Anthony. I recall driving with several of my compatriots in a snowstorm through the deserted streets. From his residence in Paris, the ayatollah Khomeini had called for a series of general strikes, which were being widely heeded. Worst of all, electricity supplies were frequently interrupted, and we were often freezing in our houses as boilers failed to work. The ambassador began by painting a very bleak picture of the political developments. He expressed his gravest doubts that the shah's regime would survive.

This announcement was received with expressions of resignation by some and anger by others. I recall one of the participants that fateful morning stating that in the event of the total collapse of the regime, he would likely have to dismiss 15,000 employees. What was Sir Anthony going to do about it? he asked. 'This must not be allowed to happen!' he insisted.

Another asked what kind of regime might replace the present one. To this very pertinent question, Sir Anthony was unable to offer any useful suggestions or reassurances. He later wrote in his memoir[1] 'Why did I, with all my experience of the region, fail to see what was about to happen under my eyes?' In his reply, Sir Anthony admits that his failure to foresee what might happen and what might follow was the greatest failure of his diplomatic career. Paradoxically he admits that his own wife had warned him, and he openly admits that his wife foresaw what he did not.

---

1 *The Pride and the Fall: Iran 1974–1979*

Mahin continues:

A few weeks later the shah left, and I was in no doubt that Iran would now slide into a dystopian nightmare of murder and profound misery. That the great mass of the people – much of it then still illiterate – welcomed change was easy to understand, but that large sections of the intelligentsia also welcomed it and could not see the danger is something that to this day I find very difficult to accept. 'How can so many apparently intelligent people be so stupid?' I asked myself.

My own brother-in-law, who was in command of one of Tehran's police stations, narrowly escaped with his life. He explained that after holding out against and killing numerous revolutionaries in a gun battle that lasted several days, he and his officers finally ran out of ammunition. Knowing that surrender would have led to their certain execution, they climbed onto the roof of the police station and escaped across the rooftops into an adjacent house, where they were able to shed their uniforms and walk safely home in borrowed civilian clothes.

Khomeini finally arrived in Tehran in triumph on 1st February 1979 and was acclaimed leader of the Iranian Revolution.

Having failed to convince General Jahanbani to intervene and stop the revolution, my only other opportunity would have been to convince my brother-in-law, General Mustapha Seyed-Javadi, to lead a squadron of jet fighters and turn Khomeini's Air France plane around at the Turkish border or shoot it down. But tragically he had died from cancer just two years earlier at the age of 44. When Khomeini finally arrived, I threw another apoplectic fit, and what I did with my family Koran cannot possibly be recorded here.

To this day, I fail to understand why so few – so very few – of my compatriots were able to anticipate and foresee the dystopian, cataclysmic events that would inevitably follow. Some of my misguided Iranian friends compared the fall of the shah to the fall of Louis XVI in the French Revolution. To my mind, a more accurate European comparison would be the fall of the Weimar Republic in 1933 that subsequently led to the outbreak of the Second World War, except that thankfully Khomeini did not have the weapons and resources that Hitler had, since he would surely have used them. The only obvious similarity to the French Revolution was that many supporters of the *ancien regime* failed to realise that their lives were in imminent danger, including most notably the shah's former Prime Minister, Abbas Hoveyda, who retired to his house in north Tehran to read Agatha Christie's crime stories, only to be arrested and summarily executed.

One of the great paradoxes of the revolution was that so few people really understood what Imam Khomeini's real intentions were. The great mass of the population believed that he would bring about social justice and an end to corruption. Much of the intelligentsia and many of the students who supported the revolution believed that Iran was about to become a wonderful Western democracy and that once the shah's regime was removed, the mullahs would hand over power to the people's elected representatives and retreat to their seminaries in the holy city of Qom. The Iranian *Tudeh* (communist) party believed that by some miracle, power would be bequeathed to them, while the Mujahedeen-i-Khalq (People's Mujahedeen) believed they would be able to introduce some form of democratic Islamic communism. How wrong they all were.

In my eyes, Imam Khomeini had so much in common with my great ancestor, Hasan-i-Sabah, but was even more ambitious in his determination to plant the Shia flag of Islam all over the Middle East and even beyond. Like Hasan, he would unsheathe the *Shia weapon* and provoke a real war with Iraq and a proxy war on the USA and Israel. What I did not foresee was that, just like Hasan, he and his successors would begin by attempting to establish – by stealth or proxy – a Shia crescent stretching from Tehran to the Mediterranean. And he would do all this while the West still believed Soviet communism to be a greater threat to western security than Islam. Only with the fall of the twin towers in New York on 11th September 2001, even though not causally linked to Iran, did Western leaders at long last begin to take seriously the real danger posed by militant Islam.

John continues:

The revolution brought in its wake total chaos throughout Iran. In the weeks that followed, almost all expatriates packed their bags and left the country. As the fortune teller's final prediction came true, that we were destined to travel the world, I was fortunate to find work in Chicago that lasted almost 18 months. From there we moved to Nigeria, whose oil revenues had quite paradoxically been boosted by Khomeini's cutbacks in oil output, where I worked for a Belgian contractor building roads, but following the oil price decline in 1982, work there came to a halt the following year. In 1984 we moved to Gabon for the construction of the Trans-Gabon Railway, which was completed at the end of 1986, when we returned to the UK. In 1990 we moved to Paris for the construction of Euro Disneyland, and finally in 1993, I found work in Brussels that lasted until my retirement in 2008, at which point the fortune teller finally left us in peace, and we returned to England.

Looking back over my career, I still feel an inextricable bond with Iran and its people. Iranian hospitality is second to none. I have been blessed with two sons who proudly consider themselves half Iranian, as well as being especially grateful for all their wonderful mother did for them in her lifetime.

In my own case, having spent 50 years married to an Iranian, I sometimes think of myself as a man with an English body and a half-Iranian soul.

EPILOGUE

I sent my Soul through the Invisible,
Some letter of that After-life to spell
And by and by my Soul return'd to me,
And answer'd 'I Myself am Heav'n and Hell'

Omar Khayyam

John:

In February 2020, following a long battle with an incurable lung condition, Mahin passed away in hospital. I vividly remember that one of the walls of the room in which she died was decorated with a colourful painting of a cypress tree, bent but not broken by the wind, as vividly immortalised in the Paisley motif, whose origins are allegedly linked to the Zoroastrian faith.

After 50 years of married life, I expected to experience an extended period of mourning, but to my astonishment, it was quite brief. Rather, I sensed the lifting of a huge weight from my shoulders.

Only when I discussed this with various of her Iranian relatives did I begin to understand what had really happened 50 years earlier. Over the years, I had learned that metaphorically speaking, Mahin's instinctive reaction to the malign influence of Islam on her life had induced her to wrap herself in a psychologically protective shell. But only now did I realise the implications. Gradually it dawned on me what had actually occurred that fateful night when I asked Mahin to marry me. She had effectively opened a small aperture in her metaphorical shell and let me in. Convinced – emotionally at least – that I was safely hers, she had irreversibly slammed the door behind me and thrown away the key. I was never to be allowed out! On her death, the shell had broken open, and I was able to step out, freed from the confines of her virtual prison. After all those years I felt like an emperor with no clothes emotionally naked and extremely vulnerable. Moreover, I realised that I had paid a terrible price for our intimate relationship. Love and passion Mahin had given me by the bucketful, but I had spent 50 years in a marriage devoid of any convincingly genuine affection. That had been the consequence of her locking me inside her shell and the sacrifice I made in exchange for the love of this stunningly beautiful and talented woman.

Looking back on Mahin's life, my enduring recollection is of a highly intelligent, beautiful human being with such a strong character she would better have been born a man. Her greatest talent was in judging the characters of the people with whom she came into contact. She possessed an uncanny ability to add people up almost on sight. That is a very rare and valuable quality in anyone. I doubt she ever really met her match in her unrivalled ability to negotiate a deal, and I certainly never saw anyone pull the wool over her eyes. Her commercial instincts were beyond the pale, while her ability in driving bargains became almost legendary among her family and friends.

There were moments when I felt privileged to be her husband. Indeed, I was very proud to have such a beautiful woman as my bride, but I never convinced myself that we were really suited to be husband and wife. In perfect marriages – if such exist – the strength of character of the parties to the marriage should, ideally speaking, be balanced. Frequently, one character is stronger – but not necessarily more or less intelligent – than the other. Where one of the partners is both highly intelligent and also possesses a strong character, as in Mahin's case, for the marriage to be sustainable, her partner also needed to be intelligent but either a weaker character, or at least be endowed with a more sympathetic and forgiving nature. Could that have been me? At best, our marriage was in lopsided equilibrium and therefore subject periodically to considerable strain. But so strong was the shell Mahin had built around us, it was able to resist all these internal forces.

Like so many of her compatriots Mahin was free with her tongue but kept her cards close to her chest. Even in our most intimate moments, I was never quite sure what she really thought about me. She was an infuriatingly private person, yet somehow her colourful personality and enormous sense of generosity made her intensely lovable.

In so many other ways, her personality was typically characteristic of so many Iranians. She was very proud and would invariably react with a razor tongue to anyone who criticised her, even when on occasion she was manifestly in the wrong. When circumstances dictated, she could be obstinately illogical, deceitful even to the point of being despicable, but nonetheless delightful and amusing. I can recall occasions when – in European eyes at least – her behaviour could be embarrassing to the point of being almost loathsome. She invariably demanded respect, but she didn't care whether or not she was liked.

There were also moments of sheer hypocrisy when, while professing the profoundest contempt for every ordinance of Islam, nonetheless she would hold her family Koran in her hand in such a way as to permit it to fall open at random so as to enable her to find a solution to a question she desperately needed answered. In a country that has a long history of actually creating and reforming religions, it is hardly surprising that Iranians have a propensity towards – if not indeed a profound belief in – their own spirituality and the merits of metaphysical speculation.

But why me? Why was I drawn into this story? Have I not been the victim – or beneficiary – depending on one's point of view, of an Assyrian clairvoyant's prediction come true?

While writing this memoir, I decided to seek answers to two difficult questions that have always troubled me. Firstly, what had provoked me to propose to Mahin so spontaneously, impulsively and unpremeditatedly? Could a fortune teller do that to a man? Could I have fallen so blindly in love that I simply lost control of my senses? For all that it is a very romantic idea, I still could not come to terms with what happened that fateful night.

Secondly, why had I been so weak, so feckless even? So many times, prior to our marriage, genuinely terrified as I was of the commitment I was about to make, I had wanted to extract myself from my seemingly involuntary promise. Given the differences in culture, in our personal circumstances, as well as the very real obstacles to such a union, however much we may have been in love, why did I not have the strength to walk away? It wasn't that our decision to go through with the marriage was intrinsically wrong or necessarily stupid, but for both of us, the personal sacrifices required were immense. Given that perfect marriages – so the saying goes – are made only in heaven, all marriages involve an element of compromise, of give and take. But the compromises inherent in this love match were hugely challenging. Is it inevitable when we fall in love that our emotions triumph irreversibly over our better judgement?

One answer to this question came quite recently from our most indignant elder son, Cyrus, when I suggested to him that perhaps his mother and I should not have married. 'Good heavens, Father, are you trying to deny me my birthright? Had it not been for the fortune teller, I would not have been born!' He sounded just like his own mother speaking. The tone of his voice inferred that the fortune teller was vested with more than power to accurately predict future events, but also the power to make her predictions come true!

In 2015, I met up with a long-standing friend who, intrigued by this story, mentioned that his sister was a trained psychologist, psychic and astrologer with a remarkable track record of unravelling such baffling questions. This led me to contact Maureen Williams. This is her response:

In December 2015, John invited me to examine the synopsis of this work. He drew my particular attention to two points that have given him great difficulty in either understanding or believing

- *Firstly, that the fortune teller's predictions turned out to be absolutely correct in every detail; and*
- *Secondly, his conviction that on the night he proposed to Mahin it was not he who was speaking, but someone inside him.*

Many years ago, people lived simple lives, adhering simply to the culture they were born into without questioning. 'Fate' was in fact an acceptance of whatever was decreed or required, and not the version of the word in modern parlance. So, I intuited that very many centuries ago, a young woman of good birth fell in love with a young man who was from a different culture – but this love match was never to be fulfilled because she was destined for a suitable marriage. She was unable, because of her culture and upbringing, to promise herself to this man because her situation made it impossible. Consequently, they both went their separate ways; their love remained unfulfilled until the day they died.

I believe that the strength of this passion led

them to make a solemn vow to hold on to that love forever. My investigation leads me to the conclusion that these events occurred in the 12th century, which quite remarkably coincides with the life of one of the most remarkable characters described in the book, Hasan-i-Sabah himself.

The strength of the vow and the circumstances in which it was made has been imprinted in the souls of generation after generation as an unfulfilled promise and has miraculously unfolded again as described in the book. In this particular case, the vow was revealed because of a 'chance' meeting – and interestingly a prediction to Mahin by the fortune teller to prime her, in a way, for what was going to happen. She and John accepted their love with very little questioning, and found a way to marry, because this was what Fate had intended all along.

The fortune teller only plays a small part in this story, but such an important one in setting the scene for the forthcoming drama! Many psychics have this gift, but their clients are often unable to hold on to forecasts completely outside their familiar lifestyles. If beyond their understanding, they are put to one side as 'unlikely'. But this fortune teller has made real history.

MAUREEN WILLIAMS
Retired Consultant, BAPS
Brit. Astrological & Psychic Society

ACKNOWLEDGEMENTS

The author wishes to acknowledge the help and support received from Maureen Williams in untangling the apparently unexplainable. Those readers who may doubt the veracity of her evaluations would be well advised to read her book entitled *Good Vibrations: Clearing Spaces and Creating Harmony* (Athena Press), which is a fascinating account of the spiritual world and its relation to our own.

John is especially grateful to Josephine Galvin who, with much enthusiasm and considerable dedication, undertook to get inside Mahin's head and partially redraft the narrative I had written on Mahin's behalf. Finally, Josephine edited the entire manuscript.

During the drafting process of this work, I have spent much time reading and studying Iranian history, most especially the legends and stories of the Ismailis. Several of the relevant books are listed in the bibliography below.

I would also like to mention Vladimir Bartol's great,

inspirational literary classic and brilliant allegorical paradox *Alamut* (North Atlantic Books), first published in 1938, presented as a historical novel about the 11th-century Ismaili leader Hasan-ibn-Sabah. The parallels that may be drawn between Bartol's profound understanding of the causes underlying the threats that led up to the Second World War and Mahin's prescient foretelling of the incipient Shia threat to the stability of the entire Middle East in particular and to Western civilisation in general following the Iranian revolution of 1979, I consider truly remarkable.

BIBLIOGRAPHY AND FURTHER READING

The Persian Encyclopaedia www.persepolis.nu

A History of Iran Empire of the Mind by Michael Axworthy (Basic Books)

A Year amongst the Persians by Edward G Browne (Adam & Charles Black 1893)

Land of the Turquoise Mountains: Journeys across Iran by Cyrus Massoudi (I.B. Tauris 2014)

The Valleys of the Assassins by Freya Stark (Modern Library)

The Castles of the Assassins by Peter Willey (Linden Publishing)

Eagle's Nest Ismaili Castles in Iran and Syria by Peter Willey (I.B. Tauris in association with the Institute of Ismaili Studies London)

The Assassins by Bernard Lewis (The Folio Society London)

The Secret Order of Assassins: The Struggle of the Early Nizari Ismailis against the Islamic World by Marshall G.S. Hodgson (University of Pennsylvania Press)

The Ismaili Assassins A History of Medieval Murder by James Waterson (Frontline Books)

The Assassin Legends Myths of the Ismailis by Farhad Daftary (I.B. Tauris)

The Wind in my Hair My Fight for Freedom in Modern Iran by Masih Alinejad (Virago 2018)

Days of God: The Revolution in Iran and its Consequences by James Buchan (John Murray Publishers 2012)

Romance and Revolution A Leap of Faith at the Iranian National Ballet by Clair Symonds (Mantua Books 2012)

The Persian Bride A novel by James Buchan (The Harvill Press 1999)

This book is printed on paper from sustainable sources managed under the Forest Stewardship Council (FSC) scheme.

It has been printed in the UK to reduce transportation miles and their impact upon the environment.

For every new title that Troubador publishes, we plant a tree to offset CO_2, partnering with the More Trees scheme.

▲ MORE TREES
LET'S PLANT A BILLION TREES

For more about how Troubador offsets its environmental impact, see www.troubador.co.uk/sustainability-and-community